# We never
# had any trouble
# before

# We never had any trouble before

A HANDBOOK FOR PARENTS
ON SUBJECTS INCLUDING:
APPEARANCE, DRUGS, LIVING TOGETHER,
COMMUNICATION, DIVORCE, DISCIPLINE,
HITCHHIKING, RUNAWAYS, SEX,
SUICIDE, RESPONSIBILITY,
AND ETHICS

## Roger W. Paine III

STEIN AND DAY/*Publishers*/New York

Thanks are due to the publishers for permission to reprint excerpts from the following:

*Cat's Cradle,* Kurt Vonnegut, Jr., copyright © 1963 by Kurt Vonnegut, Jr., used with permission of Delacorte Press/Seymour Lawrence.

*Go Ask Alice,* Anonymous, copyright © 1971 by Prentice-Hall, Inc. Published by Prentice-Hall Inc., Englewood Cliffs, New Jersey.

*The Magus,* John Fowles, copyright © 1966 by John Fowles. Published by Little, Brown and Company, Inc., Boston, Massachusetts.

*The Rainmaker,* H. Richard Nash, copyright © 1954 by H. Richard Nash. Reprinted by permission of William Morris Agency, Inc.

"Twenty Tips to Parents from Parents" first appeared, in somewhat different form, in the June, 1974 issue of *Parents' Magazine.*

*Library of Congress Catalog in Publication Data*

Paine, Roger W
We never had any trouble before.

1.  Adolescent psychology.
2.  Adolescent psychiatry. I. Title.
BF724.P33      155.5      75-8896
ISBN 0-8128-1833-4

For my father:

A man of few words,

who always means every one of them

Grateful thanks to the S. T. McKnight Foundation for a grant which made the completion of this book possible; to David Stanley, who believed in it when it was still only an idea; to the hundreds of parents and young people whose experiences are the essence of all the pages that follow.

# Contents

# Foreword

"We've never had any trouble before with any of our children —not until now." A father has just told me that his youngest daughter has run away from home; they had argued earlier in the evening over his disapproval of her new friends in school. He is still feeling bewildered because he was sure something like this couldn't happen in his family.

Most of today's family problems do not happen in problem families—they happen to good parents with families that never have any trouble, at least not any serious trouble. This is a book for families like that. It is written in the spirit of "preventive maintenance," but it is also full of suggestions for dealing with parent-teenager conflicts and with crisis situations, should you ever have to face them.

It is harder to be a parent of teenagers today than ever before, and harder to be a teenager as well. And although college campuses have their lively and their lazy years, the time between thirteen and seventeen is never very calm. The most valuable virtue in those years is patience. I have known a great many young people with deep troubles—the girl who has run away from home for the third time in six months; the boy heavily into drugs; the young couple on their way to a New York clinic for a secret abortion. I am still in touch with many of them now, two to five years later. They are doing things like making high grades in college, or making six dollars an hour on a construction job, or assistant managing a small boutique—the full gamut of life's good possibilities are represented. They seem to have turned out as they did regardless of whatever happened back in their troubled days.

Of course a gentle word here, a pointed remark there, a pat on the shoulder or a kick in the rear can do a world of good when they are timed right. And having those nudges or not having them adds up, either to a feeling of support or a feeling that nobody cares. But if the kind word or the swift kick is missed occasionally, either because of insensitivity or fatigue or surrender, I have a feeling that in the end it won't make that much difference. We are a resilient breed, we manage to live through our teenage years, and if they are happy years we're lucky. If they are hard, self-doubting, lonely years, then welcome to the club. We've still got all kinds of time to make up for them—which is one reason why I never begrudge anyone a second shot at adolescence, even when it begins at forty.

Many parents with teenagers who are in trouble will ask, "What's normal, anyway?" In any family, what is normal is to fumble, to guess, to use discipline when it shouldn't have been used, to be nice when sheer meanness would have been better, to hesitate a year too long for that frank talk about sex, to have a communication breakthrough at a time when you least expect it, to hear her say a total of ten words from her thirteenth to her fifteenth birthdays, and to feel enormously proud when he brings home his first "A" ever—just when you had given up hassling him about his grades.

The family experiences which illustrate this book occurred between 1967 and 1973. Those were the years of Vietnam, drugs, dropping out, long hair, a flash flood of runaways, and a raised, clenched fist. They all came at once, and we had no time to sort them out, to step back and get some perspective. Out of those years comes a stockpile of family experience in the midst of crisis: how parents and teenagers handled differences that were often new and confusing to everyone.

Times have changed but the problems have not, and that is why this book is full of anecdotes based on real family experiences. It is a book about human beings, and for that reason it is not always a consistent book, because what works for one person does not always work for another.

I have a friend from my early years, Margo, who always knew whenever her mother brought home a new book about how to understand teenagers. Margo would sneak the book, read it from cover to cover, then put it back on her mother's bedside table. That way she always knew what to expect, "what they're going to try on me next." During her years of conflict with her parents, I often longed for a book openly intended for them all.

I hope this can be such a book. I have addressed it to you, the parent, but I think there is much in it that will be both interesting and profitable to teenagers.

In every family dispute I have ever seen, things got better only when the seeds of healing were already there—in both the parents and the teenagers. And those seeds are nearly always already there: sometimes they need water, sometimes they need sun, and sometimes a little of both. In that sense, this is a book about sun and water. The events in it are real. The names are my own invention, to safeguard the privacy of the real people behind them.

—Roger Paine

# 1

# What's Normal?

When I think of normal life I think of the fifties, the silent fifties, those years when I was a teenager growing up in Old Virginia—the Eisenhower Years. Memory commonly misrepresents the past and my memories are only those of a young boy, but I recall those years as a time when life was simpler, goals were clearer, change went forward at a moderate pace, and most people knew right from wrong. It's ironic to think that Elvis was brand new back then, and many parents wondered if it was entirely moral to allow their children to listen to his records, much less watch him perform.

Beer was quite enough in those days if you were a high school student itching for a wild Saturday night, and those of us who were lucky went gladly off to college where everyone studied and partied in normal proportions.

Then came the sixties. Could there possibly be two more different decades? The sixties were strange and singular years, occasionally shrill and often tragic, years when idealism was both expressed and acted on. And, for perhaps the first time in history, youth became not an age but a movement. The changes outraged some people and excited others, and none of us are quite the same after living through them.

Today we seem to have a curious mixture of values from the fifties and the sixties, and those of us who were teenagers during the fifties are now or are about to be parents of teenagers. Many other parents who already had teenage children during the late sixties are now watching their youngest children turn thirteen and, if you are one of these parents, perhaps you wonder how the next few years will be similar to and different from the most recent past.

We *are* in the middle of a partial return to the style and the values which started in the mid-sixties, when college students spat in year-end proms in 1968 discovered that the students wanted a prom in 1973, and the trend continues. Beer is back too. The trade schools have long waiting lists. A bleary-eyed student has been studying, not planning a new demonstration.

I remember the complaint of a frustrated father back in 1969: "Thirty years ago when I was a boy, I'd look at my father and say, 'Anything you can do I can do better!' But today, my boy looks at me and says, 'Anything you can do I don't even *want* to do!' "

Few fathers have such a complaint today. The revolution of values which started in the mid-sixties, when college students spat in the face of the profit motive, has come full circle; the chief goal of today's average college student can typically be summed up in three words: to make money. The idealist is still around, but today he is the exception rather than the rule. Maybe the economy has scared us so badly that even our kids feel insecure, but if it is normal to want to make lots of money, then we are having a return to normal times.

Even so, the seventies are hardly a perfect renaissance of the fifties; the years in between have changed us permanently. Marijuana will never return solely to ghetto hideaways. The birth control pill will continue to make sex safer and easier for everyone, including single young people. Growing up will never again be as simple as it once was. We have lost that sense of working together for the good of our country that so many people felt during the fifties and the early sixties. We have been struck by a series of dreary, consuming events during the first half of the seventies, and we have allowed ourselves to become rather self-indulgent and escapist as a result. All of this is having an enormous impact on our children.

We have with us a legion of aging cynics from the late sixties, but we also have hundreds of drug treatment centers, youth hotlines, street counselors, teen clinics, free schools, and runaway centers we did not have before. The problems which inspired these services are not going away. The reason, as one sharp sixteen-year-old girl put it, is that "there are a lot more ways to be bad now." There are certainly a lot more choices available to kids * today, most of which make young life much more complicated. One of these choices, for good or ill, is

## THE BIRTH CONTROL PILL

The pill is available today at hundreds of Planned Parenthood clinics and free teen clinics across the country. Each clinic treats from a few hundred to several thousand young people every year with the help of volunteer doctors and nurses. Not all teenagers come to the clinics for birth control; minor medical treatment, pregnancy tests, testing and treatment for venereal disease, and general physical examinations are also part of the program at most clinics. The major drawing card is confidentiality. The kids come because they don't want you, their parents, to know what's going on, at least not right away.

The very presence of teen clinics changes the lives of young people today. Confidential access to effective birth control gives them a choice which didn't exist ten years ago: safe sex. The old, practical reasons for avoiding sex no longer apply. Before the pill came along, sex among single young people was both a moral and a practical question. Kids had to ask themselves first, "Is it right?" Then, if they got past that one, they had to ask, "What about getting pregnant?" Today they face only the pure moral decision, and the clinics are full of teenage girls who want to go on the pill.

A few parents believe that if the teen clinics didn't exist, the sexual morals of young people would improve. But the clinics didn't start the trend toward unmarried sex; by the mid-sixties, increased love-making among high school and college students was a national

* A distinguished friend who read this book in its manuscript form objected to my use of the word "kid"; technically, a kid is a young goat. But I dislike the word "teenager," adolescent" is textbookish, and I have yet to meet a teenager who wanted to be called a child. They call each other "kids." I have used all these words in this book, both for variety and because there are so few good words available that describe a person between thirteen and nineteen years of age. If you object to "kids" yourself, perhaps you will take comfort in knowing that English writers have used it to describe children since the time of Shakespeare.

phenomenon. A practical response was needed and the clinics were an obvious one. I think their existence does help maintain the trend toward more casual sex, but so do movies, novels, bikinis, discussions of the new morality, and history's healthiest pituitary glands.

I didn't realize how sheltered my own adolescence was until I started working with today's teenagers. I was a true follower of the Puritan fathers; I didn't kiss a girl until I was seventeen, didn't touch a beer until I was eighteen. When I got angry with my parents I took long walks, but I never considered taking long runs into the next state! That was 1958. Ten years later I would have been a walking anachronism. In some cities and suburbs right now, I would be a simple impossibility! We still have lots of good kids but not as many naive ones. The reason is that church and family could once shield children from divergent points of view, but the world is too much with us for that to be possible now. A sixteen-year-old named Karen gives us a good example.

Karen calls the Youth Emergency Service in Minneapolis, a phone service in business to answer calls from teenagers and from parents twenty-four hours a day. She wants to discuss, anonymously, the pro's and con's of virginity. After a two-hour conversation with a male volunteer who picked up the phone, Karen decides to have sex with her boyfriend. The phone volunteer, a graduate student in psychology, does not take a position for or against teenage sex; he does serve as a sounding board for Karen, helping her clarify her own thoughts, doubts, and questions.

It is not a light decision. Karen loves her boyfriend and thinks they will marry some day. She also loves her parents and knows her decision is a rejection of their strong moral standards (that sex should be reserved exclusively for marriage).

According to The Sorensen Report, a 1973 study of adolescent sexuality in America, more than half the girls Karen's age also reject their parents' ideas about sex. Even if those figures are inflated, they are a good warning light: one or more of your children are likely to reject at least part of what you have taught them, including some of the values you have stressed the most.

Karen's experience one month later at a nearby teen clinic may also give you some insight into the new life style of many young people. A nurse begins by taking her medical history, then she asks Karen a series of extremely personal questions. The nurse tries to

help her feel as relaxed as possible and Karen answers the questions
matter-of-factly.

"Are you living with your parents?"

"Yes."

"How often do you have intercourse each week?"

"Maybe once, some weeks not at all."

"Where do you have it?"

"Usually at my boyfriend's place."

"Do you have intercourse with one partner or more than one?"

"Just my boyfriend."

"If you don't get birth control here, will you continue to have
intercourse anyway?"

"I'll probably try someplace else."

After a lecture on the different methods of birth control and a
doctor's examination, Karen is given a prescription for Demulen.
Not all clinics ask the same questions, but most are concerned about
parents who think clinics are encouraging sexual license. They ask
the questions so they can be sure they are dealing with a girl who has
got her mind made up. Ironically, a virgin who comes in for the pill
may not be able to get it because some clinics will prescribe only for
teenage girls who are already sexually active. This makes sense if you
want to protect yourself against irate parents, but it doesn't make
sense if you're trying to help a girl who plans to have sex and wants to
be sure she won't get pregnant!

Karen's story ends sadly. Her mother found the pills, and she was
told to stop seeing her boyfriend. Although Karen had never lied to
her parents before, she began lying so she could see her boyfriend.
Six months later the romance ended of its own accord. But the
climate around her house was permanently changed; Karen had
stopped talking with her parents about anything very important.

Karen is not part of a small minority of freethinking high school
girls. She is, in fact, an engaging, energetic girl who teaches Sunday
School to third graders in her church, a girl any parent would be
proud to have. Her story raises all kinds of serious questions which I
want to put off until later; for the moment I want only to emphasize
that life is more complicated for young people today, that more
input is available to them than ever before, and that Karen is very
much like all "normal" teenagers.

More liberal attitudes toward sex among young people are not

our only heritage from the sixties. Middle-class high schools are still
the best places in town to buy

## DRUGS

Marijuana and other street drugs have created a new society in
the schools, a freak society with its own unique kind of prestige.
Status no longer depends on your ability to be (in descending order of
importance) a football hero, a basketball or hockey star, a cheerleader, a student council officer, the valedictorian of the class, or the
newspaper editor. Of course, an exceptionally handsome or beautiful
student can gain status on looks alone. But until drugs came along,
those were the traditional and the *only* ways to get attention in high
school, and if you couldn't make it, you were just one more ant
among thousands.

Different kids use drugs in very different ways. In many high
schools, you will find at least three types of teenagers using drugs.
First, there is a small cadre of introverts. They often limit themselves
to marijuana and hashish, shunning alcohol and "unorganic"
chemical drugs like LSD, amphetamines, and barbiturates. Next
there is a large, middle group of kids—extroverts—who also stick
mostly to marijuana but are experimentally minded; they will try
something different if persuaded by a good friend. Unlike the introverts, who are likely to smoke dope several times a week, this
middle group sticks to weekend use, usually at parties. Good athletes
are part of this group, along with a cheerleader or two, and a large
cross section of any high school's student body. The last group is a sad
one; kids who indiscriminately use drugs on a daily basis. They will
come to school stoned, dare you to bust them, and in the end they
often drop out.

The worst drug abusers in teenage society are junior high school
boys. For them, high status depends on being one new drug ahead of
the gang. Maintaining this status involves lots of hard work, like
stealing enough money from mom and dad and other sources to buy
new drugs and stay high. A police bust is a special honor in this
group, and the pressure to be cool produces a new clique of hard-
core drug kids every year, kids who are literally destroying them-

selves so they can keep up their tough–guy image. During the late sixties it was fashionable to walk around saying, "I'm really burnt, man." But the glory has faded; now even the kids who enjoy drugs on an occasional basis will describe the heavy users with a term both sad and tragically apt: "wasted."

Like the new sex standards, drugs have obscured the definition of normal behavior among teenagers. Parents are settling for less than they used to; Chuck's story is a good example of this.

He began using drugs cafeteria-style when he was only fourteen, taking anything he could get his hands on except hard narcotics, which he both feared and couldn't afford. By the time he reached ninth grade, Chuck was injecting speed and downers. The speed he bought from friends, the downers he took right out of the family medicine cabinet and melted them down into a solution he could put into a syringe. An amazing number of teenagers get their drugs from medicine chests in their own homes and those of their friends. In Chuck's case, his father was taking tranquilizers because he had been feeling anxious about a business deal as well as his son's drug problem.

The family saw a psychologist who helped Chuck's parents but failed to help Chuck. They finally stopped going, and two years later Chuck gave up drugs in exchange for Colt 45 malt liquor. Why? "I just got tired of being so spaced out." All his friends had made the same switch. Best of all, "the cops don't hassle us for drinking beer." Today Chuck comes home drunk on beer almost every weekend, but when his parents compare the past with the present, they feel relieved. I think they are relieved because alcohol, unlike street drugs, is something they can understand. They would rather have a drunk son than a stoned son.


## THE EXPERIENCE GAP

Parents in the past have always been able to look at their children and say, "Anything you've done, I've done—or at least I've thought about doing it!" The well of our wisdom has always been fed by the springs of past experience. If Johnny staggers home drunk one night, Dad reacts on the basis of his own boyhood memories, memories which often include a similar escapade. He may punish Johnny, have a long talk with him, or look the other way, depending on the pull of his own inner experience.

But drugs have changed all that. Marijuana and LSD are not part of the background of most parents, and so they present a unique problem—a lack of parallel experiences. Dad knows what to do if Johnny is drunk, but he doesn't know what to do if Johnny is stoned. He wonders, "Do I call the shrink, the cops, or the hairy guy running the local youth center?"

Teenagers are having experiences today which their parents have never had, and the result is a peculiar kind of "experience gap." Drugs are not the only reason for its existence. A teenage girl who hitchhikes has experienced a side of life that, chances are, her mother never has. Popular music is another new experience; music itself is an ancient art and today's parents have their own pop tunes, but total immersion in electronic sound at one hundred and twenty decibels with twenty thousand other people in a huge arena—that is likely to be a totally new experience. It is also a bone of contention in many families because some parents (ear specialists in particular) are reluctant to give their teenagers permission to attend large rock concerts.

This lack of parallel experiences is the main reason why it's harder to be a parent of teenagers today than ever in history, and the experience gap is likely to be with us for a long time. For one thing, it is beginning to cut both ways; conservative parents are often frustrated by liberal children who want to try new experiences, but the liberal kids are growing up, having children of their own, and the world is standing on its head. It's entirely possible that we will be seeing parents who believe in marijuana with kids who think the stuff is terrible; parents who *want* their children to live with a lover before marriage arguing with kids who think that cohabitation is immoral; and kids running away from home because their parents won't give them any rules. That may sound far-fetched, but in any shopping center you can already see mothers wearing jeans and a poncho, accompanied by daughters in knee socks and a jumper. It's rough being a parent either way!

## LANGUAGE

Traditional parents have a hard time with the way kids talk these days. I once asked two hundred and fifty adults to respond to this question: "What trait among young people today is most objectionable to you personally?" As possible examples of unpraiseworthy traits I listed long hair, old clothes, sexual attitudes, the use of drugs, political ideology, and the use of vulgar language. Long hair and old clothes came in last; at the top of nearly everyone's list was vulgar language. Apparently the public use of four-letter words goes against the grain of a value as old as civilization: simple good manners.

Swearing is not the predominately male sport it once was, and this is what bothers parents most. When I was in college we planted a microphone in the ladies' room at my fraternity house during a big weekend. Those were the days when young ladies and gentlemen were discreet about their public conversations, so we were curious about what the girls had to say when no male ears were nearby. When we listened to that tape on Monday, most of our ears turned deep red. Many an ego suffered for weeks in the wake of the absolutely candid appraisals dished out in the ladies' room and captured by that impartial microphone.

The use of four-letter words in mixed company is still considered crude by many people, but most young people and a growing minority of adults consider it honest or "real." The double standard is down, too, which means the words are just as likely to issue from the mouth of a girl as a boy. This can come as quite a shock to untutored parents with progressive daughters. Linda is an example of the latter.

She is a shy, small-boned girl whose father has always treated her like a china doll. When she was fifteen they had a big argument and ranted and raved until their words had escalated to the shouting stage. Frustrated and emotional, Linda yelled, "What do you care? You don't give a shit about me anyway!"

A tense but total silence followed, like the moments before a bridge collapses. Then her father slapped her hard, so hard she can still feel it when she tries. She spun around, walked slowly to her room, and locked the door behind her.

Linda's father had never struck her before; he had never heard her swear before, either. His image of Linda was shattered, but he felt immediately ashamed of himself for using physical violence. He set about the task of getting acquainted with the real Linda, the daughter underneath his superficial image. In the following weeks he discovered that he liked her, he liked her a lot. He could get along better without some of her ideas and habits, but he was like all fathers in that respect.

## APPEARANCE

In middle-class families, appearance is often a big issue. Barb, the second of three children in a rather well-to-do family, went to the Good Will store in November and bought a patched, navy-blue pea coat. It cost her $2.50. She wore it home and almost everywhere else until spring. Her parents were mortified, but Barb took a lion's pride in her new coat. She had gotten it herself, using her own money and resourcefulness, and it was an important symbol of her rising independence.

Parents today are called on to demonstrate far more grace under pressure than parents in the past. When Barb's parents let her wear her Good Will coat to the family reunion that Christmas, it was pure grace. They are conservative people by nature, their financial success is recent and hard-won, and it is important to them to see their children dress "nicely," as Barb's mother puts it. But when parents can recognize the symbolic importance of a small thing like Barb's coat—and refuse to let it threaten their own self-image—moments of grace become possible.

The army and navy surplus rage in clothing is waning now, but it will never die out completely. The hottest fabric is still denim, although many kids are back to letting you spend your money to buy the latest fashions. At least work shirts and old jeans were economical, which is something to consider these days. The basic lesson is that when it comes down to a battle over appearance, it's best to save your ammunition for something more important.

## HITCHHIKING

We have all read at least one horror story about hitchhiking. Some young man thumbs a ride over to a friend's house and is never seen again. A girl out on the road alone is picked up and taken to a basement apartment where she is tortured and raped. As every reporter knows, nothing grabs our attention more quickly than a tale of cruelty, and there are enough such tales linked to hitchhiking to keep them in the news.

There is a positive side to hitchhiking, though, and it's important to know what it is. Hundreds of thousands of young people have seen America from one end to the other using only their thumbs for transportation, and this cross-country odyssey is often an excellent maturing process. Most kids have never had a bad ride and only a fraction of a percent of all hitchhikers ever have a fatal one. And the lasting effect of a hoof-and-thumb view of the country seems always to be the same: the kids come home with a new love and respect for this land.

But for most parents, the grisly images cancel out the good side. The result can be a running feud with one or more of your teenagers. A compromise is possible, and you can work toward it by asking your itchy-thumbed teenager a few questions. Such as: how well can you defend yourself if you should get an obnoxious or a potentially dangerous ride? One girl who had hitched almost daily for three years had one bad experience during that time; a man with sex clearly on his mind tried to take her to a deserted section of woodland. When she saw what he was doing she told an astute lie. "You might as well forget it, mister. I've got v.d." His jaw dropped, he looked over at her, and then proceeded to drive her where she wanted to go.

Ask your teenager: could you be that resourceful? Could you keep your wits about you? Do you know which streets in town are safest for hitchhikers? Which are the most dangerous? You aren't likely to find an ideal solution, but an open discussion starting with some of these questions might point you in a direction you can live with.

One interesting issue which is often linked with hitchhiking is the desire among increasing numbers of high school graduates to take a year off between high school and college. Most parents want to see their kids go straight to college without delay, and therein lies the rub.

An eighteen-year-old leaving high school is like a bird on the wing; the world stretches out below him and he wants nothing more than to glide along, landing from time to time in the field of his choice. His life is, for perhaps the first and final moment, totally his own. He can hitchhike, climb mountains, volunteer to work for a public service agency, retreat to a forest cabin and write a novel, or live in a strange city and discover what it means to start alone, at the bottom. All too soon he will have to settle down to a life defined by grades, promotions, vacation days, overtime, and a multitude of other responsibilities. It is no wonder that some kids want a year to do nothing but roam free.

When your teenager isn't ready for college, sending him despite his feelings is a waste of your money and his time. College performance depends on motivation, and motivation comes only when we have some vision of what to do with ourselves. A year off to think about the future is usually an excellent investment, both for teenager and parent. If you're afraid he or she may fall into the extended vacation syndrome, a good compromise is delayed admission. The prospective student makes a tentative decision about college, talks with the admissions people, and begins his year off between high school and college with a guaranteed place in a particular college one year hence. Admissions staff people at many colleges and universities are even willing to help plan a "stop-out" year away so it will be as meaningful and productive as possible.

## JUNIOR HIGH KIDS

Reinhold Niebuhr, the theologian and social theorist, wrote a book entitled *Moral Man and Immoral Society*. His thesis is that when an individual becomes part of a group, he often bows to the morality of the group, even when the group commits an act that goes against his personal morals or inclinations. It is an explanation for the lynch mob, and it also explains why you should never sit near a group of junior high kids in a movie theatre.

They are at once the most winsome and curious, the most exasperating and destructive people I know. They are too young to be sophisticated and too old to be cute. They are capable, within the space of a single half-hour, of both remarkable energy and infinite laziness. Taken one by one they can be enormously likable, thoughtful, and amusing. Running in a pack, they can get profanely and revoltingly drunk, insult half the town, and break the radio antennas off a block's worth of cars.

Although some of this behavior is "normal" for junior-high-age kids, it is still just as hard to take. Parents need to be in touch with what kind of behavior to expect from kids this age; you'll want to be able to judge what is par for the course against what is not. Kids in their early teens are great attention-needers. The boys develop a slow swagger to go with their new too-tough-to-care philosophy of life; the girls may wear lots of eye liner, and hang around with the boys in front of the corner drug store chewing gum. They can all swear—even the innocent-looking ones—like construction bosses, and they go to all this trouble because they want people to notice them. I am stereotyping, of course, but you probably recognize one of your own kids, which will be normal.

You will probably be left out of the most intimate thoughts and schemes of your junior-high-age kids. You may have to resign yourself to being the enemy for a year or two or three because you (who else?) will be the one reminding them that they still live in a world where order, rules, and expectations abide. Your lone comfort may be the guarantee that, in time, this too shall pass. Your biggest problem may be the feeling that one or more of your early teenagers is

## GROWING UP TOO FAST

A fourteen-year-old girl today can easily appear to be nineteen or twenty; she may even have a college-age mind to match her figure. She is given away only by her emotions, which usually shuttle along a track between ages three and thirty. If she displays Kissinger-like diplomacy one day and screams door-slamming insults the next, she is behaving normally because she is rather innocently caught at the mid-point between child and adult. We have all had to cross that point ourselves, and a few of us have re-crossed it a time or two.

The great danger for every young person gifted with intelligence and early maturity is the temptation to use this gift to manipulate parents and friends. For a girl named Julie, the fruits of successful manipulation were too sweet to surrender. She is a straight-A student, she can talk for hours on an informed, vivacious level about dozens of subjects, and she is equally skilled at a three-day sulk. Until a year ago, the end result of whatever she did was always the same: she got her own way.

Devious methods are usually adult weapons. The best route to disarmament is to use other, less calculating adult weapons: honesty, straight talking, and common sense all make a good start. Julie's life changed for the better one night when she got so drunk she was unable to hide it from her parents. They sat her down and peeled away the half-truths she had fed them for months. Three afternoons a week she was supposedly practicing art after school but in fact was always at an older boy's apartment. At other times she was rarely ever where she said she was going to be.

The problem for her parents was control and trust. Can we trust her again? Do we really have any control over what she does? How can we get her to tell us the truth in the future? They decided to treat Julie as a young adult. They refused to give her orders or to decide the rules for her behavior. Instead they discussed her hours, their expectations, and the importance to all of them of maximum truth. (They knew that no normal teenager tells her parents everything.) The rules they set were mutually agreed on, and physical punishment was forever banned; obedience to the rules was to be the basis for mutual respect. Julie was thirteen when all of this happened.

She slipped up a few times, just as any person will unless immaculately conceived. When discipline was necessary, it was discussed between father, mother and daughter, with Julie deciding for herself what the punishment should be. She was always a bit harder on herself than her parents would have been.

These days many kids seem to be growing up too fast and the temptation you will face is to hold them back, to give them a few more years of childhood; it is a natural temptation and, considering the obligations of adult life, it is an honorable one. Nevertheless, when your teenager has, even as early as twelve or thirteen, something close to an adult mind and body, you will serve him well if you decide to treat him more like an adult. He isn't too young to learn that freedom and responsibility come in a single package.

Down deep, what is normal about adolescence is what has always been normal. Loneliness. Feelings of inadequacy. Elaborate attempts to hide loneliness and insecurity behind brave fronts. Boy or girl problems. Confusion. Occasional hassles with parents.

We've come through a time when kids asked hard questions about everything they saw: the school system, American foreign policy, police ethics, the dominance of assistant principals, the power of parents, and the relevance of the church. Kids today are still asking questions, but they are no longer using bullhorns to do it.

The kind of life you live still depends very much on *where* you live. A seventeen-year-old girl remembers this picture of young life in a Chicago suburb: "In sixth grade, girls were wearing nylons, make-up, skirts up to their butts, smoking cigarettes. They were already growing up and going first and second with the boys behind the plaza. I can remember going home and crying because we had just moved there. Where we had come from, kids were just kids."

So what's normal? The only thing we can say for sure is that normal is a risky word; it depends a lot on what you've been through. "I think parents forget they were once a kid," says a young man who works full time. "They get an ideal notion of what their kid should be like: you never get in trouble with the police, you don't drink, you don't smoke, go to bed at 10:30, do well in school. And all of that is great, but just think what kind of a person that would be! That would be the weirdest person you could run into!"

Something weird that may become normal in the next few years is a vision of the future in a play called *Tango*, by Polish writer Slawomir Mrozek. The three central characters are a mother, a father, and their young son. The parents are graying hippie types with long hair, Bohemian clothes, love beads, and no apparent livelihood. Their son marches around the cluttered living room as if he were on a drill field, dressed immaculately in a dark blue pinstripe suit. He can't stand his freethinking parents, and they can't stand him. To paraphrase Bob Dylan, the times keep right on a-changin'.

# 2

## Getting Attention

I was trying to outline a talk I had to give later in the day, and my office was full of noisy afternoon visitors, all young friends from two nearby high schools. It seemed like a fine opportunity to gather some fresh ideas.

"I've got to give a talk tonight. The people want me to tell them 'what teenagers are thinking about these days.' So what do I tell them? What *are* you guys thinking about?"

Everyone laughed, several faces went blank, several others furrowed with concentration, and then one of the initially blank faces lit up:

"Getting high!" a boy said with a foxy grin. That set off a chain reaction.

"Getting grades," said another boy with the solemnity of an acolyte.

There was a stage whisper from over in the corner: "Getting laid." That brought snickers and an eyes-to-the-ceiling look from one of the girls.

"If Bob or Jean were here, they'd say, 'Getting with the Lord.' " Raucous laughter. This was a group of hardnoses, and no one liked the God Squads.

A tall brunette with a writer's collecting, sorting mind summed it up: "It all boils down to getting attention—one way or the other."

Precisely. And the group had already mentioned four of the five major ways that young people (together with most of the rest of us) get attention: drugs, grades, sex, and religion. Add sports and the list is almost complete. Suicide is a sixth way, and the suicide rate among teenagers is rising. Since kids rarely have the confidence to come right out and say, "Pay attention to me, please!" they *do* something to attract attention, something they are good at. If they aren't good at anything, then they may get themselves into trouble because even negative attention is better than no attention at all.

Sometimes people need attention more than food and shelter. Attention is milk for the soul; it is not a luxury but a necessity of life. If I don't get a little every day from someone, I start feeling sorry for myself, but I know there are good kinds of attention and bad kinds. In my world, good attention is a smile, a backrub, a compliment from someone who doesn't give them often, or a long letter from an old friend. Bad attention is an unpaid bill, an unfriendly stare, or a parking ticket on my windshield.

For a teenager, even worse than bad attention is no attention at all, the weight of the world's indifference. Getting no attention is like being immersed in a colorless, odorless room-temperature liquid.

Kids need attention from friends, relatives, teachers, and a member of the opposite sex. Most of all they need attention from you—their parents. This need ebbs and flows throughout adolescence, and although pride prevents most young people from admitting it, the need is always there: your presence at a ball game, your praise for a job well done, your help on a tough algebra problem, your opinion about sex, your willingness to listen.

You may feel tempted to say, "Oh sure, my kid wants my attention—pointed the other way!" And sometimes that's true; no teenager wants to be watched, coached, and praised constantly by his parents. But the great dilemma for every teenager is that he is a secret schizophrenic. One part of him wants ultimate freedom, the other part wants ultimate security. One side of him says, "I don't give a damn what you think!" and the other side says, "But I need you to believe in me!"

So let's look more closely at the six ways in which young people get and seek attention, and at what you can do to pay your own attention in a careful balanced manner, enough to satisfy but not to smother.

## SPORTS

Robert Redford, if you're interested, has declared that the only true test of a man is the foot race. But my high school days as a half-miler never got me anything except leg cramps and a gradual penchant for solitude. No crowds ever came to watch a track meet; the cheering was all reserved for the football, basketball, and hockey teams. I'm not at all bitter about this because I'd much rather watch a football game than a track meet myself.

I particularly like the junior varsity football games. The boys are just learning, so the play is always a bit sloppy. I wind up watching the fathers shouting from the sidelines more than the teams on the field; the fathers are a lot more interesting.

"Hang in there, Tuck! Smash him harder next time! Stay with him, boy!" Gunmetal hair, Budweiser gut, forearms like sirloin tip roasts, he is bellowing at number seventy-nine, who doubtless will be the Alex Karras of 1986. The father reminds me of Woody Hayes. A less vocal father tags along with Woody, both of them roaming the sidelines with every play. Father number two doesn't say much, but he's there—and his son knows it.

The stands are full of parents, mostly mothers since it is four in the afternoon on a Thursday. Woody Hayes turns out to be an insurance salesman: "Sure, I miss a sale now and then if the client can't wait until Friday morning," he says. But Woody never misses a Thursday afternoon on the sidelines, yelling encouragement to his son.

I know a mother who attended every soccer and hockey game at her son's high school. He had barely made either team and rarely got to play, but he practiced like a true believer. When the coach did put him in, his mother was there in the stands, and though I never heard him admit it, you could tell it was important to him.

Parents with athletic sons are often keenly aware of the importance of being there to watch. But just as teenagers can get used to getting attention in only one way—say sports—parents can get used to giving praise for only one kind of achievement. Excessive devotion to any single activity produces a one-dimensional person. The varsity athlete who cares about nothing else, partly because his parents praise him for nothing else, is like a dray horse with blinkers on; he sees only what is straight ahead and misses all the richness of life passing by on either side. I don't mean to pick on athletes. The bookworm, the Jesus freak, the doper, and the star halfback are all the same person under the skin. They see only the coming exam, the potential convert, the supply of grass for the weekend, or the goal line thirty yards ahead.

Our behavior is never coincidental; it exists because it is reinforced, and you can use this fundamental truth about human behavior to widen and enrich the lives of your teenagers. For example, what if Joe averages twenty-five points a game during the basketball season? He probably gets a lot of praise for an average like that, and he gets it from all kinds of people: his girl friend, his teammates, his coach, the newspapers, and his parents. Now, what if Joe brings home a C in English? He may have had to work hard for that grade, but chances are he won't hear much praise for getting it. If, on the other hand, you do praise him for the C in English, talk with him about the course and encourage him to try for a B next quarter, you will nourish another side of his personality. The object is not to produce a perfectly rounded human being at the age of eighteen, but to open some new doors just a crack. A C in English could also be Joe's very best, and in that case you don't push him to do better, you just reinforce the C with lots of praise.

Now and then a good high school athlete will suddenly, and without apparent reason, give up sports entirely. In situations like this, parents are often very athletic about jumping to conclusions. Most parents assume that their sons have traded in their uniforms for a hash pipe. Actually, boys have dozens of reasons for quitting. They want to bring their grades up so they can improve their chances for admission to college, or their coach is hassling them about long hair, or their interests have simply and innocently changed. One young man didn't play football during his senior year despite daily pressure during the month of August from his father and from his coach. The reason he quit, a reason he never shared with them, was that he had two good friends who were in deep trouble and needed him for support.

## GRADES

Four times a year Debby waits until dinner is over, the dishes are washed, and her father is settled into his favorite reading chair. Then she approaches him like a coquette.

"Want to see my report card, Dad?"

Her father puts the paper aside, looks at his oldest daughter, and realizes he can't remember just when it was she stopped wearing Fruit-of-the-Looms. He is a busy man, well known and respected in his profession. Sometimes he has to ask his wife a question like "Is Debby pretty?" He is both too close and too distant from her to know for sure, and is a little surprised when his wife answers, "Of course she is. What are you, blind?"

He takes the packet of slips and inspects them one by one with the care of a jeweler squinting through an eye loupe. He is not surprised that each card, as they all have since he can remember, boasts an A.

"Your teachers like you better every term," he says. "You're really the smartest one of us all." He has a warm smile for her, but he doesn't hug his daughter as he would like to because he isn't sure what the rules are for showing affection to a daughter once she is showing signs of becoming a woman. Debby's father wants to be supportive but, like the athlete's father who shouts his encouragement from the sidelines, he knows only one way to show his affection; he praises her for her grades.

I suggested that he try complimenting Debby for her looks from time to time, just something simple like "You look good in that outfit," or "Your hair looks great today." Simple sincerity is the only rule. He followed through on this suggestion and two weeks later, when I saw Debby on the street, she gave me a glowing fifteen-minute report about how good she felt because "my dad actually broke down the other day and told me I look nice!"

I have known smart kids like Debby who discover they can get more attention out of poor grades than they ever got with straight A's. They will sluff off for a semester, deliberately fail a class or two, and then wait for their parents to react. They don't do this in hopes of getting more praise in the future for better grades, but because they are not reinforced in other areas of their lives. You can help prevent this kind of behavior simply by watching your teenager's actions and reinforcing the activities which you appreciate but to which you normally pay little attention. Giving good attention can be as simple and easy as a single sentence, something like "That was really a good job you did on the back lawn today." It's simple, but it is also one of the most powerful forces known to man.

## SEX

Speaking of powerful forces, I'd like to tell you about Mary, a girl who collected boyfriends just as sucessfully as Debby collected A's. She was only fifteen when a casual boyfriend asked her if she would like to "do it" with him. Almost as an afterthought, she said, "Why not?"

Mary was a virgin, the boy meant little to her, and the experience she had that night fell far short of the book versions she had been reading. So why did she do it?

When she was fourteen, Mary was like most teenagers; she was extremely self-conscious, insecure, and quick to respond to anyone who showed an interest in her. She was intelligent, but she felt no interest or support coming from her teachers. Her parents were unhappy together and so busy with their own problems that they had no time left over to pay attention to her inner needs. She was also pretty enough to attract attention from boys, and in fact they were the only people in the world right then who made her feel good about herself.

So one year later she said, "Why not?" And after that night it was as if she had jumped and was living in a long fall. During the next two years she went to bed several times with several different boyfriends, each of whom would take her out for a month or two and then drop her. After a while, Mary's attitude toward sex was "What difference does it make?"

Mary's parents got a divorce when she was a senior. By that time she was using drugs heavily and had a reputation in school as "an easy lay." No one was particularly surprised when she took an overdose of seconal, and that was part of Mary's tragedy: her cynical friends felt that she "would do anything to get attention."

The attempted suicide forced people to take Mary seriously enough to put her into a treatment center. It was the best thing that had ever happened to her. With daily attention and supervision, Mary got a handhold on self-respect. About six months later she came home, and several professionals were waiting for her with a tailor-made program designed to keep her well. In the group were a couple of school teachers, a juvenile officer, one other counselor from my agency, and myself. Normally Mary's mother and father would have been the most important part of any plan to reinforce the good feelings she had gotten while in treatment, but neither parent was strong enough at that point to be much help.

Phase one of this post-treatment program involved getting Mary to keep her pants on when the boys came after her body. Her reputation in school had not changed during the time she had been gone.

"You know your old boyfriends are going to want to take you to bed," I told her—and she nodded "yes"—"so you're going to have to show them that things are different now. Do you think you can do it?" She promised to try, fearful that this austerity program would lose her every potential boyfriend in school, but more fearful of falling once again into a pit of self-hatred. As she succeeded in saying "no," we praised her, congratulated her, and encouraged her to keep it up. Her self-respect grew stronger with every passing week.

Phase two of the program involved school. No one had ever encouraged Mary to apply herself, to read books, to take a look at what she might want to be in the future. Her teachers gave her a lot of support, and she began using the mind she had always had. She deserved the attention and the good grades which came as a result, and it made her feel marvelous. She began thinking of college, an idea that had never before crossed her mind.

Is it too simple to say that Mary got well because she got good attention? Or that her life fell apart in the beginning because she didn't get the right kind of attention at the right time? Watching her make her comeback was gratifying to me, but I couldn't help thinking about what had brought her down so low in the first place.

## RELIGION

Connie is short and stout and covered with freckles, a girl whom her mother described on the phone as "heavy" and "very insecure." She joined the Jesus Movement when she was a high school junior, a decision which pleased her parents at first but then gave them cause for concern. "She is getting to be impossible to live with," her mother said, "and when I ask her about where she goes and what she does with all her time, she just says, 'You wouldn't understand, mom.' "

There was much more meaning behind the words "You wouldn't understand, mom," than Connie's mother realized. Connie's two sisters were slender, attractive, popular in school, and had always gotten lots of attention from everyone, including their mother and father. Connie had grown up with a self-concept so low that you couldn't even find it when you talked with her. She felt ignored by everyone, so she ate too much and failed to apply herself to anything. It was as if she had determined to make herself as ugly and as useless as everyone seemed to think she was.

Then some kids in school invited Connie to a meeting for Jesus People; more than sixty students were crowded into a large basement recreation room in the home of one of the school football stars. The leader of the group was in his early twenties, a college student who looked like Ryan O'Neal with a beard. The meeting started when he strummed John Denver's "Follow Me" on a guitar and everyone sang. Even Connie, who had never liked to sing. It was the first time she could remember feeling simple joy, without any inhibition whatsoever.

The leader's name was Gil. He gave a short talk on loneliness, a talk which moved Connie because she knew a lot about loneliness, and then it was over. There was no invitation to "come forward and give your heart to Jesus," no heavy revival meeting pressure; the meeting was left open. The kids who had invited her asked Connie how she had liked it and asked her to come back the next week.

Two weeks later, Connie stayed for a long talk with Gil, and that night she "found the Lord" and became "a born-again Christian."

To begin her new life, she tossed out all her make-up, a picture of herself taken the year before, and thirty books which she now considered too much "of the world." Among them was Hemingway's *The Old Man and the Sea*. She also gave up the only life goal she had ever seriously considered, a plan to get a degree in psychology and work with retarded children. Now she wanted to enroll in a Bible college and spend her life winning converts to Jesus.

Sports can distort the life of a good athlete, grades had distorted Debby's life, sex had distorted Mary's life, and religion, in this case, distorted Connie's life. She spent two years with the Jesus People before she realized that her life was so narrow it was hardly any life at all; she had reached the point of thinking about other people not as people but only as potential converts. She had used Jesus to fill big holes in her life, holes created by the indifference of other people, including her parents. Today she is glad the movement was there to rescue her and she is glad she got out of it when she did.

Connie plans to spend her life working with lonely people, and one of her favorite stories involves an old woman who wanders into a young minister's office in Manhattan because she couldn't stand sitting alone in her apartment for another hour.

"And don't sit there and say that Jesus loves me, young man," she warned the pastor. "When you're old and alone like me, that's not good enough anymore."

## DRUGS

Because so many parents are frightened by the talk about street drugs, using them has become a perfect symbol of youthful rebellion and a good way to get attention from parents who haven't reacted to anything else. The problem is that the more attention drug-using kids get, the most encouraged they are to keep on using drugs. This is especially true for junior high school students.

Mike spent all of his junior high years running with a group of hard-core kids who had reached the needle stage of drug abuse. During the first week of our friendship, I saw three different Mikes. With his parents he was snotty, selfish, and indifferent; with his friends he was self-assured, clever, and a natural leader; with me he was intelligent, witty, and considerate. But drugs were at the center of all three of Mike's personalities.

Mike and Mike's group were the talk of the community. They got special attention from the police, school officials, parents, assorted angry neighbors, and from counselors like me. And they *loved* all this attention, they wallowed in their notoriety; what we were doing was simply reinforcing the very behavior we deplored.

A basic law in behavior therapy is that you must *totally ignore* the behavior you want to extinguish and reward the behavior you want to see strengthened. Several different professionals had been able to develop a strategy to help Mary when she came home from treatment, but no common strategy could be devised for Mike and his peers. It was too much to expect the police and the school officials to ignore Mike's drug use, even though they realized that they might inadvertently be reinforcing his delinquent behavior. On the theory that half a loaf is better than none, I convinced Mike's parents to ignore him when he came home stoned or when he made any mention of drugs. The other half of their job would have been to reward him whenever he said or did anything they liked, but attention is not always a reward; in Mike's case, he liked to get attention from me but despised attention from his parents. It was a stage he had to go through, and in order to help him his parents swallowed their pride and waited.

During our twice-weekly talks I ignored Mike when he tried to talk about drugs and encouraged him when he talked about a book he was reading, a girl he had met, or a class he was enjoying. But as the months went by, his drug use continued and, if anything, seemed to get worse; the callow glory of so much police attention was too powerful. If one of the kids got arrested, that made matters even worse because an arrest was such a badge of honor.

It seemed that Mike would have to go one of four ways, depending on the whims of fate and his own character. He might fall in love with a girl who would be strong enough to pull him away from his drug use; love is still the most powerful force of all. Or he might be converted to an equally powerful peer group like the Jesus People. A third possibility would be the simple passage of time wherein drugs might begin to bore him as he matured and thought more seriously about his future. And finally, he might graduate into an ever-harder drug scene which, in the end, would make him a certified addict.

The real Mike fell in love with a girl who didn't return his feeling and the disappointment fueled his drug use for several months. Then during his junior year his self-pity changed to self-disgust and he cut down on drugs to an occasional marijuana high. It is impossible to say exactly what brought Mike to that partial but fortunate decision. Once we might have looked back on two or three difficult years and said, "I guess it's just a stage some kids have to go through." But no parent is willing to think so philosophically about two or three years of drug use by a son or daughter. Nor should you.

Mike's critical years came between his twelfth and sixteenth birthdays. They are years of self-appraisal and self-doubt, of hope and humiliation, of needing help and refusing to admit it. A growing number of kids are failing to get the attention they need through sports, grades, sex, religion, or drugs; some of these kids will commit

## SUICIDE

Picture this experiment. A dog is harnessed into a box with a wire grid for a floor. In front of him is a hurdle which he can't reach because of the harness. A painful shock is sent through the grid. The dog leaps and howls, struggles and growls, urinates and defecates uncontrollably. But the shock continues no matter what he does, no matter how hard he tries to escape it. After a while the dog gives up. He sits helplessly, motionless on the grid, taking the constant pain without a sound.

Now the harness is removed. For the first time it is possible for the dog to change his situation, to get away from the shock by jumping over the hurdle. The shock begins again but the dog does nothing; he sits silently, just as before, and takes the pain. Psychologists call this "learned helplessness." If a trainer with infinite patience and skill spends months helping him over the hurdle, showing him that it is possible to get away from what hurts him, the dog will finally learn that his life need not be defined by pain. But it will take a long time to convince him.

I think teenagers on the verge of suicide are often in a state of learned helplessness. They feel that they are harnessed into an intolerable situation and believe that no matter what they do, their life will not improve. Tunnel vision prevents them from working to change their circumstances—they see no light at the end of their particular tunnel. They may see the hurdle in front of them, but they are convinced that the effort required to jump it will be useless.

You can find a dozen elegant theories that explain suicide. Pay no attention to them. At the bottom of them all are sadness and pain, and you don't need a theory to understand that. Something in the marrow of our society has tripled the suicide rate among teenagers in the past ten years. Suicide is now the second leading cause of death for kids, and if the actual numbers are still modest—perhaps 10,000 fatal attempts by teenagers last year—the numbers aren't the point when the stakes are so high. Suicide rates in other age groups have leveled off or declined recently, but the rate is rising for teenagers.

The circumstances which lead to teenage suicide do follow some predictable patterns. More black and chicano kids commit suicide than whites. A teenager who has lost a parent by death is more likely to make a serious attempt on his life than a teenager who has lost a parent by separation or divorce, but both are more likely to consider suicide than a teenager living in a healthy two-parent family. The most common pre-suicidal symptoms are severe depression and moroseness, withdrawal, loss of interest in much of anything, irritability, and neglect of personal appearance. But I have talked with kids on the day before they made serious attempts and noticed no unusual depression, no certain giveaway signal. In fact, if a person makes a definite decision to end his life, having the decision behind him may make him seem happier: he knows how he is going to deal with his problems. Young people who attempt suicide are often intelligent, sensitive, and mature beyond their years. Their decision to die is usually touched off by the loss of a lover, or the inability to win a lover, or by a failure to live up to parental expectations.

Girls attempt suicide much more often than boys. They generally use pills or cut their wrists. Very few of them want to die, perhaps two percent of the total who try. If they do die it is usually an accident—too many pills, too deep a cut, or an expected rescuer who is unexpectedly delayed. But the dejection, the pain, and the feelings of helplessness that lead them to try suicide are real; their attempts are not merely a dramatic game.

Tammy was fifteen when she cut her wrists at a weekend party.

She had taken a lot of barbiturates and was drinking heavily, and that combination might have killed her if she hadn't built up such a strong tolerance over the previous several months. The problems troubling her that night—the loss of a parent, failure in school, self-disgust caused by her recent, frequent drunkenness—would not be pushed away by the music, the attention lavished on her by boys, or the anesthetizing effect of the drugs. She went to the bathroom, cut deeply into her wrists and let the blood flow. The cuts were long and deep; she would have died in there if someone hadn't broken down the door.

Although boys attempt suicide less frequently than girls, they succeed much more often. They tend to use more lethal methods such as guns, or a rope. Despite this earnest choice of weapons, most boys don't want to die either. But at the moment they make the decision, they are serious.

On a winter's night this past year, a boy walked alone into the middle of a large field. Scarcely more than 200 feet away, the lights of dozens of homes were visible through the bare trees. If you had been able to ask him then, he could have given you the names of several of the families who lived in those homes. He lay down, folded his arms, and after a while he must have slept. The temperature was below zero, and when found he was dead. Apparently he wanted to die. The one truth we must accept is that no power on earth can force a person to live when he chooses to die.

Kids thinking of suicide will almost always tell at least one other person. That person is not likely to be a parent. Unless you or your teenager are most atypical, you will be shut out of the inner world he creates around himself in the weeks or days before suicide. So your involvement will probably begin only after the fact. You will see your child in the hospital after her stomach has been pumped or his wounds bandaged. You may have to bury him and then find a way to sort out what happened so you and your other children can go on with your lives. You will need to be concerned with the impact of one child's choice to die on your other children. Suicide is not genetic, but it does run in families—children who have seen a parent or a sibling use it as an answer will be more likely to use it themselves than children in families with no history of suicide. If it happens in your family I suggest inviting someone, a friend, minister or counselor, to help you and the other members of the family work through your feelings.

Actually the chances are very high that should one of your children attempt suicide, the attempt will fail. Fatality occurs for one boy of every three who makes an attempt; for girls, the ratio is one of every ten or twelve. You are likely, then, to be faced not with a burial but with the survivor of a deliberate attempt to stop living. What you say and what you do will be very important.

Did you ever have the experience, when one of your children was small, of thinking he was lost somewhere and perhaps badly hurt? Every siren on the street is an ambulance taking him to the hospital. You pace and worry, you call all the places he might be, you imagine the worst, and after hours of being on edge you find him at some friend's house, oblivious of your concern. You don't know whether to cry with relief or shout with rage.

You will feel that precise mixture of emotions if one of your teenagers attempts suicide. Relief, and then anger. The anger is just as appropriate as the relief; after all, your kid has thumbed his nose at you and at the rest of the world. But don't let your anger cause you to say things like "You shouldn't have done that" or "You didn't need to do that." Later on, looking back, you might say, "It really made me mad when you tried to kill yourself," and saying those words will be a good thing. Anger means you care. You wouldn't feel it if your child didn't matter to you. So tell him—after a few days—how you felt when you heard about his attempt to kill himself. Many kids commit suicide partly because they don't know how you feel, because to them, it seems that you don't really care what they do.

Your teenager probably won't want to talk, especially with you, about what he has done. He will continue to shut you out to an extent, and you're bound to feel frustrated and hurt by this. I have worked with several teenagers who attempted suicide, and most of them wanted to talk about something other than the fact that they had just tried to kill themselves. Don't push for answers and details your son or daughter is not ready to give, and may never be ready to give.

At the same time, *show that you are willing to recognize what has really happened.* It was not an accident, not a mistake, not a foolish impulse, not a meaningless gesture. Although there is deep ambivalence in every suicide attempt, especially among teenagers, any such attempt is a serious statement. The chances are your teenager did not and does not really want to die, but he does want to see some reasons to live. If he says, "I feel worthless," resist your temptation to tell him how great he really is; you don't want to deny the feelings he is sharing with you, but to ride with them for as long as it takes to get them all out. It is so important to let him talk his feelings through, and your primary role is that of the active listener. Later there will be time enough to say, "I think I understand how you feel, and I also see some other things about you." Then tell him what you like about him.

If you get a chance for a talk like that, you are a rare parent. You may have to resign yourself to the fact that you will not be allowed to play the part you want to, that you will have to find someone else to do the listening and the talking, at least in the beginning. There are more than two hundred Suicide Prevention Centers in the United States today. Use the one nearest you for direct help or for a reference.

Several years ago a friend of mine who is a child psychiatrist made a grim and astute prediction. He said that when kids got tired of drugs, they would turn to suicide. Drugs were merely a temporary way of avoiding the issues that suicide can permanently resolve. The past several years have seen his words come true. The rest of the seventies will see a continuing increase in the number of teenage suicides.

I think the reason for this is that kids today don't know how to struggle with pain. Most of us have had to struggle many times with the emotions that lead to suicide: disappointment, loss, failure, despair, loneliness. But we have protected our children from such struggles too often when they were small. We are also living in a decade which, so far, is escapist to the core. It is no wonder that teenagers have found so many shallow ways to avoid the struggles which they must embrace if they are to grow. They have used drugs to cover up pain and music to drown it out. They have had movies designed to help them forget, and even their religious leaders have absolved them of the struggle by suggesting that Someone Else has done it for them.

One of my favorite plays is Tennessee Williams' *The Night of the*

*Iguana,* a scene from which seems relevant here. Shannon, a minister who has lost his church and is on the verge of a nervous breakdown, has come to a rundown resort in Mexico. He is "spooked," and he needs time to gather his wits about him. He meets Hannah Jelkes, a New England spinster who has been on the edge of panic herself but has always found the strength to defeat her "blue devil," the name she has given to that which frightens her most.

"How do you beat your blue devil?" asks Shannon.

"I showed him that I could endure him—and I made him respect my endurance. Endurance is something that spooks and blue devils respect. And they respect all the tricks that panicky people use to outlast and outwit their panic; everything we do to give them the slip and so to keep on going."

Kids today are not learning how to endure, how to outlast and outwit their panic and pain in ways that their personal blue devils will respect, in ways that build up the spirit and lend fiber to the soul. And so, when a young person is struck, as inevitably he must be, by the difference between what he hoped to be and what he is, he feels absolutely lost, without purpose, a dog on a grid taking the shock without motion or sound. He is still too young to accept a compromise with life but he is now too old to shrug off the reality of his own limitations. We have not prepared him for that moment, and he has missed many chances to learn on his own.

As parents, we can start a counter-trend by allowing our children to fight their own battles from a very early age, win or lose. We can insist that our kids face life squarely. We will do this best when we do it by example, refusing to hide from them our own struggles with disappointment and pain; rather, let the battles be fought openly. We can provide a comforting shoulder when they lose out on something or someone that mattered. We can say, "I love you no matter what you do." And we can refuse to make excuses for them or to spoil them with empty praise. Finally, we can ask that they work hard to find a purchase on happiness that depends not on something artificial like a drug, but on a person, a place, and a sense of purpose.

We all hit a mid-point in our growing years when it is not clear, even to ourselves, whether independence is our pose or our truth. The great test for all parents is to accept a teenager's independent pose as his truth, yet leave room for his dignified retreat, for a return, if necessary, to the unconditional security of home. It is a hard test. To let out the rope of freedom a proper number of lengths. To feel the rope strain, demanding still more freedom. "Shall we let Cindy go to this outdoor rock concert over in Wisconsin, John? It's all weekend, you know." To say "yes" when you want to say "no," because although "yes" will make you nervous, it will also give Cindy a chance to prove herself. Finally, to have the grace to let that same rope be used, if need be, as a lifeline back home. To do all this and to do it so that the young dignity of your son or daughter is never abused, never given an "I told you so," at least not by you. Most of us are exposed soon enough to the jeers of our old ambitions.

It's one thing to know that kids need a lot of attention and will do most anything to get it. It's quite another thing to be able to offer love and attention in such a way that they are accepted by a son or daughter who needs your guidance and at the same time needs to rebel against you. The art of "getting through" is as varied as the people who are good at it. Describing what I've seen work, in the next chapter, will give me a chance to introduce to you some of my favorite people.

# 3

---

# Getting Through

Some people like to touch and be touched and others simply don't. An open show of affection is natural for one person while another is more comfortable when emotions are reserved for private times. Plain talking is this man's strength, but that man prefers indirection, perhaps a gift as a way of saying, "You are important to me." And all of us express ourselves through our actions, which is often the most eloquent and convincing form of communication.

An old law of communications theory declares that we cannot *not* communicate. We are always sending out messages with our words, actions, or bodily posture, even when we don't mean to be. And there has been a rash of new theories in recent years telling us how to say what we really mean to say, how to get in touch with our real feelings, how to own up to what we feel. I don't want to offend any enthusiasts for these new theories, but I do want to put forward a modest proposal of my own: when you want to say something important, you will probably have your best results if you stick to whatever comes naturally. Expert theories can be a little threatening, if not dangerous, when they ask you to use a method of communication which goes against your grain.

It is easier to get through to other people when you are relaxed, and it's hard to relax when you're trying to fit yourself to someone else's theory. If hugging isn't your thing, for instance, why worry about it? Whether you realize it or not, you already have your own style of communication, your own unique way with words and facial expressions. Your way will work best for you precisely because it is *your* way.

This is a chapter full of examples of parent-teenager communication. They are all different because they happen in the lives of different people; however, they do have one quality in common: simplicity. You will see as you read on that a simple act is not necessarily an easy act; that the simplest word or gesture can require a noble measure of thought, courage, and patience. A good example is the importance of

## ACCEPTING THE SECRETIVE YEARS

Between their thirteenth and fifteenth birthdays, most teenagers say very little to their parents; "pass the butter" is usually par for the course. These secretive years may come earlier or later depending on how quickly your children mature. One fourteen-year-old may seem genuinely secretive while another just seems busy all the time, but if you sometimes feel you are getting the silent treatment you should be neither surprised nor concerned. The silent years are also years of awakening, as natural and as necessary as the hushed and luminous hour before dawn.

Have you ever heard a teenager say, "Everyone understands me but my parents"? Those words, a common refrain, are also a positive sign of growth. They are ironic words as well, because your kids may not be giving you much of a chance to understand them. But that's okay because, if you remember your own early adolescence, you know how important it is to begin putting some distance between yourself and your parents. Some parents who are both clever and wise look at their fourteen-year-olds and do understand—but they pretend that they don't!

Some young people really like high walls. They build careful and noticeable walls because they want to keep some of us out and attract others to look in. A girl named Emily had walls like this; whenever I asked her a question about herself it was like dropping a rock down a deep well and never hearing the splash. Finally I stopped asking personal questions, I gave her all the space she wanted, and we spent a few months talking about nature, poetry, fairy tales, whatever came to mind. Then one day she said, "I need to talk to you about something important." A lot of kids are like Emily.

Most teenagers do enjoy talking with adults, but the adult has to be someone other than their own mother or father. You may find that even when your own teenager won't talk to you, someone else's teenager will—which can present you with an ethical dilemma. Claire, thirteen, liked to have long talks with the woman for whom she babysat, a close friend of Claire's mother, who is a warm and open-minded person in her own right. Although Claire rarely said anything of importance to her mother, she shared with her mother's friend her feelings about school, sex, drugs, the Republican Party, and the strength of her parents' relationship. More than once, this good woman wondered if she should be sharing some of the wealth with Claire's mother.

Your best solution to a predicament like that is to clear your feelings through Claire. "I think what you just told me is something your mother would really enjoy hearing from you. What do you think?" If Claire says no and if you still feel strongly that her mother should be let in, say so—and promise Claire that despite your feelings, your own lips are sealed. It isn't always easy to be a young teenager's confidante, but your first loyalty is to the precise definition of that word: "A close, trusted friend."

Teenagers need to put some emotional space between themselves and their parents, but at the same time they need an empathetic adult ear so they can share the excitement and the frustration of moving toward maturity. If a young teenager still shares his secrets with his parents, he is merely postponing the period of self-definition for a later time. That time will come, indeed it must come, unless he is to be a carbon copy of his parents or an eternal mama's boy.

## THE ACTION THAT SPEAKS LOUDER

"Do as I say, not as I do" is a parental refuge we had best declare inoperative. Many parents are finding that troubled kids start getting better when they see their parents go to work on their own problems.

Kathy was fifteen when she "started doing dope, hitchhiking, going out to different towns to meet people, and staying away from home over every weekend." She used speed heavily during school:

"It would get me through the day, because I couldn't stand school."
She also liked LSD and marijuana, even cocaine when she could get
it. Part way through her tenth-grade year, Kathy quit school. The
oldest of three children in an upper-middle-class suburban family, a
long, lean girl with lively dark eyes, she might have grown up to be a
model or a philosophy teacher, a magazine editor or a psychologist,
but at age fifteen she chose to be a drop-out.

During Kathy's worst drug years her father was an unadmitted
alcoholic. Father and daughter had always been close, but his booze
and her dope anesthetized their affection and respect for each other.
As the months went by and Kathy was at home less and less, as a last,
desperate measure her parents signed her into a nearby hospital for
treatment.

"It was a waste of money," Kathy says in retrospect. "I split
twice from the hospital and went thirty miles to see some friends, got
high, then went back to the hospital about two in the morning."
Released after four weeks, she returned to the old friends and habits
she had never seriously considered giving up and spent very little
time at home.

Then Kathy's father decided to come to terms with his own
problems; he committed himself for treatment as an alcoholic. It was
a courageous move, and when he came home even Kathy could see
the change in him—and that was when she decided to get well. She
needed no residential treatment, no out-patient counseling; her resolution was enough. She spent her last two years in high school
"straight."

First-born children often identify with their fathers. They may
emulate their father or struggle to be his exact opposite, but either
way they shape themselves with father in mind. Since Kathy had
chosen to be like her father, when he changed his script, she changed
hers. His decision to stop drinking might not have had the same
dramatic impact on one of the younger children in the family, but for
Kathy it was like an irresistible challenge: "If I can do it, you can do
it." Today her life is as fresh and promising as a clean canvas.

## CLOSENESS THROUGH CONFLICT

Shaw wrote, "If you strike a child, take care that you strike it in anger . . . " I don't recommend that you strike your teenager at all, angry or not, but Shaw has hit on something very important. An angry person is a person who cares. Being mad at someone takes a lot of energy, energy we would save for someone else if we didn't care so much.

Rick never felt close to his stepfather while he was growing up. "I really resented him when he didn't care about being at the father-son banquet for Boy Scouts, or when he didn't show up when I was playing a Little League game—stuff like that. It got to the point where, when I was a junior in high school, I didn't relate to him at all. I related to the guy at the grocery store more than my father."

As he grew into his teens, Rick's conversations with his father were usually arguments. "He really disliked long hair, but it was a stylish thing for me to do, it was an 'in' thing, a fad, and it was what I wanted. As far as he was concerned, no son was going to live in *his* house and go around looking like a hood. That's the word he used—hood."

Most of Rick's friends had stopped getting haircuts whether their parents liked it or not, but Rick kept after his father for permission to let his hair grow. Finally he got a grudging okay: "You can grow your hair out, but you're not going anywhere with me." Rich shot back, "Well, that doesn't make any difference—I don't go anywhere with you *now!*"

So Rick's hair grew down over his ears to his shoulders. He always kept it clean and neat, but the longer it got, the clearer it became that his father had not honestly reconciled himself to a son who "looked like a girl." "Are you going to set your hair tonight?" was one of his favorite cracks at the dinner table.

Harassment between parent and teenager can be like tossing live grenades back and forth; someone may be hurt badly enough, even when the issue is trivial, to run away or to abuse drugs or to lose all contact with reality. However, Rick was unusually secure for his age and finding excuses was not his style, so one day he asked his father if they could have a long talk—about fads.

"I explained to him why I wanted long hair, that having long hair was the thing to do, that I didn't want to feel left out, and that I still liked girls as much as ever." He compared long hair to the maroon vests kids had worn when his father was young. Maroon vests! They were the thing to do back then. "And finally my father understood that I didn't want to have long hair because I wanted to be a *hood.*"

After that talk they began spending more time together. Rick showed an interest in what his father was doing, and his father began sticking up for him, even defending some of Rick's viewpoints. It was the beginning of a new relationship for them both.

A man in an encounter group told the other participants that he had never felt close to his parents. Like Rick's father, they had simply ignored him. Another man in the group said that he, too, had never felt close to his parents, but for a different reason.

"I wasn't ignored. But no one in my family ever got very emotional about anything. Somehow we all knew that any deep show of emotion would be an embarrassment. So we were always very polite to each other, very considerate. No one ever got angry, no one ever raised his voice. And none of us—well, *I* never felt close to anyone else."

We all learn to use politeness as a device to keep other people, even our own children, at a distance. The parent and teenager who can get mad, who can level with their feelings and exchange hard words if need be, are closer to each other than the parent and teenager whose relationship is one of carefully measured consideration.

## SAYING IT SYMBOLICALLY

When I have something important to say, I feel most comfortable saying it in a letter because I like the distance a letter gives me and the time I have to compose my thoughts. While I don't think this is an admirable trait, nevertheless I find the courage to say things in letters I might never say face to face. Some of us are like that, and a dozen encounter groups will never change it.

A gift is the tactical cousin of the letter. When unspoken emotions have built up, when words fail, feelings can be expressed symbolically. Here is the story, in his own words, of an independent young man who learned just that.

"The first job I ever had was in the seventh grade—I was a caddy. I started making my own money. I knew my dad couldn't tell me what to do with my own money, because I was working for it. From that time on, I've always worked, I've always had good jobs and made lots of money. So I was really independent even when I was very young because everything I had, I bought. Clothes, a towel fee at school, books for classes—you name it, I paid for it myself. I never asked my dad for a penny and I don't resent it. It's just the way I am now. I pay my own way.

"I was working in a clothing store when I was a senior in high school. I spent a lot of money on a new suit for my dad that Christmas. I bought it because he was kind of a shabby dresser; it wasn't that he couldn't afford it—he could, but he just didn't care. And I also wanted to show him that I was financially successful. I wanted him to think, "Well, that kid's not just messing around, he's *doing* something!'

"I got the suit all wrapped up, and on Christmas Eve he opened it up and just couldn't believe it. He just couldn't believe that I'd spend that much money on *him*. I gave it to him also because I wanted to, you know—I wanted to show him some kind of affection. And he broke down and started crying, because he just didn't believe I dug him at all, and I really did, even though I didn't show it a lot. I didn't want to give in sometimes, and I'm sure he didn't, either."

People who can't find the right words can say a lot in other ways, but there is a hazard for parents in that story: it is often unwise to try to turn the moral around. Kids love gifts, but if they feel you are trying to spend your way into their hearts they will resent rather than appreciate what you give them.


## SHARING INNER SPACE

As a counselor, my greatest moments of pleasure come when members of a family share deep feelings with each other—feelings they may have expressed outside the family but never inside it. At the same time, I am saddened by the realization that many parents and children say so little to each other, on their own, about real "matters of consequence."

Neil is a natural athlete who, during his ninth-grade year, gave up sports and found that he enjoyed marijuana and speed. He and his father held shouting matches in the living room three or four nights a week, arguments which were all passion and no perspective. As time went on, Neil, who has a near-genius level IQ, lost interest in school completely and ran away from home twice. His parents finally took the entire family in for counseling.

Surprisingly, Neil thought counseling was a good idea. Within a month his attitude toward his father had reversed itself; it had happened not because the therapist was a magician, but because Neil's father had talked about himself during the sessions. As part of a routine procedure designed to help the therapist get acquainted with everyone in the room, he had asked all members of the family to say a little about themselves, especially about how they had been feeling in recent months. Neil's father spoke openly about the pressures of business and about his nagging fear of failure; at times he wondered whether it was worth all the energy he was using to hold together his company, his family, and himself. This was the first time he had shared these feelings, in so many words, with anyone in the family, and Neil was mostly deeply affected. He had never heard his father give voice to any feelings other than angry ones. It was as if he had suddenly joined the human race; at least it seemed that way to a son who had never seen his father's reflective side.

Neil did not change overnight, but he took a new interest in helping around the house and worked hard to hold his temper. The old shouting matches came only once a month or so, and counseling was discontinued. The family learned to say more to each other on a deeper level as a natural part of daily living.

A family counselor can serve as a good coach or as a judicious referee, encouraging truth and calling fouls when necessary, but the basic ingredients for a closer, more open family are already part of every home. Find a time when everyone, even the youngest children, can be together; this time may come once a week or twice a month—whatever feels right to you. Then use the occasion to share triumphs and frustrations, plans for the future and feelings about the present. If you want to be super-organized about it, you can, but whatever you do, fit the style and shape of your meetings to the personality of your family.

## IT TOOK THE DISTANCE TO MAKE US CLOSE

The unwritten rule is that we keep our children until they are eighteen, then they go off to find a job or to get a college education. The separation at age eighteen often does both parents and teenagers a lot of good; when they get together again they appreciate each other more because they have a different perspective. Some parents are willing to arrange for this kind of separation at an earlier age, in hopes that it will have the same salutary effect—and most of the time, it does.

Samantha was the last of three children and the only one still living at home when she turned sixteen. Her father had died when she was only seven and, for a few years, she had been very close to her mother. But by the time she was thirteen, Sam felt the need to put space between them so she could grow on her own. "I spent most of my spare time with my friends. I would come home to eat and sleep, and sometimes exchange words with my mother."

Three years later she wanted her independence—a place of her own and the right to make her own decisions. Sam's mother wanted her at home, but not if home meant little more to her than a boarding house, so she presented four alternatives.

"You can continue living at home, of course, and go to school just as you have been. Or you can quit school, live here at home, and find a steady job. If you feel you have to go somewhere else, you can live with your aunt and uncle in Denver and go to school there, on the condition that you come home for your senior year. Of, if you want to get away from both home and school for a while, you can live with your aunt and uncle and find a job."

Four choices. Sam had never been given a chance to choose, entirely on her own, the direction her life would take. All kids like to complain about school, but if the choice is really offered—to stay in or to drop out for a while—what do you do? All kids gripe from time to time about the rules at home. Still, if the choice is right there in front of you, to leave home or to stay, what do you do? Sam took a long time to decide; she was determined to make the most of the big decision that was totally hers to make. She knew her mother wanted her to stay at home, and she had lifelong friends who also wanted her to stay, yet her instincts told her, "I've got to leave, I've got to be somewhere else for a while." So she went to Denver and to high school there.

"If anything, my relatives and I were further, much further apart than my mother and I. But I needed that. It gave me a healthy perspective on the way my mother thought, and it was a neat feeling to write letters to her."

The year in Denver was a good one for Sam. She loved Colorado, she made lots of new friends, and she learned that compared to some other parents, her mother was open-mindedness personified. She did the kind of growing that comes only from being in a new place and, although she might not consider it important, her grades that year were the best of her high school career.

Sam went home with mixed feelings, but the mixture had more to do with the new friends she was leaving behind than the home to which she was returning. "My mother and I still had our differences, but we liked each other. As the cliché goes, it took the distance to make us close."

## THE CLOSEST PARENT

Sex, natural inclinations, similar tastes, and mysteries we shall never fathom combine to draw a child closer to one parent than to the other. The first-born may be closest to father, the second-born closest to mother, or you may have normal father-daughter, mother-son ties. Or, as often happens in families I have known as a counselor, you can have a teenager who is understood by one parent but who would *like* to be understood by the other. To be aware of these inner feelings and special pairings, and to make use of them during times of tension, is to be a more effective parent.

Cindy is a gifted, sensitive, and stubbornly rational girl who has always identified with her father. He is a brilliant, sensitive, stubbornly rational man. Like scholars on a retreat, Cindy and her father often have long discussions into the night. For them, no subject is too deep, no hour too late.

Cindy's mother is impulse-made-flesh, and so is her older brother Gavin. Mother and son are clearly on the same wave length. They rarely say anything to each other, but they seem to understand, instinctively, the intentions of the other.

Normally everyone in the family gets along fine, although if Gavin is caught skipping school or Cindy wanders home at three in the morning, the drill is set: father talks with Cindy and mother talks with Gavin. Years of frustration taught these parents that Gavin won't listen to his father and Cindy won't listen to her mother, and that the kids' selective deafness has nothing to do with disrespect. Rather, it's the natural resistance of water to oil.

Gavin understands an impulsive, gesticulated volley of words because this is his own language, but it's a language that his scholarly father has never been able to learn. Fortunately, his mother is a master at it. Cindy recoils and shuts her ears when her mother starts shouting, but she listens and responds when her father, exuding the sweet breath of reason, sits her down. Again, this is her own language.

Now if we are most interested in developing rounded personalities, we must admit that Cindy could use a measure of her mother's spontaneity and that Gavin could use a touch of his father's calm reason. In a crisis, however, the discipline should be meted out and the healing oils administered by the parent with whom a teenager feels the closest rapport. The balancing of head and heart can wait for a more peaceful occasion.

The greatest danger for you as parents is that some incident will drive a wedge between you and your spouse. For example, in mother's opinion, father is too lenient with Cindy. But if you confer beforehand and arrive at a consensus, each of you can present a united front in your one-to-one talks with the kids. If, in plain fact, you can't agree on a united front, then it's time to step back a moment and discuss the pro's and con's of consistency.

## CONSISTENCY

No one is perfectly consistent, nor should you wish to be. Absolute consistency is the first refuge of a narrow mind, even though a degree of consistency is an essential parental skill. Your kids need to know that they can depend on certain things about you. So stop a minute and ask yourself: "What can my kids depend on about me? How do they know what to expect from me when they break a house rule?" Do they believe you will never budge an inch from a position you've taken in the past? Or do they believe you can be persuaded to change your mind on a past position if their arguments make sense to you? Are you consistent about punishments but inconsistent about privileges and promises? What can they count on from you? Do you tend to be more lenient than your spouse? Or are you the tough one? Or are you both in rather close agreement when it comes to rules and the consequences for breaking those rules?

In every home, some rules should be so natural and so consistently upheld that they are a part of the woodwork. In several families I know well, the teenagers always tell their parents where they are going, what they plan to do, and when they will be back. And they know that if they change locations, they should call in advance to ask permission and leave the phone number of the new place. It never occurs to the kids in those families to complain. The value of consistency is that after a while a pattern of behavior becomes second nature, like saying "excuse me" when you get up from the dinner table.

The danger of consistency is that you will be tempted to use it as a dodge. Rather than rethink an old rule, you say: "This is the way we've always done it, and this is the way we're going to do it now." It's so important to remember that your kids are growing and changing—whether you are or not! Last year's hours may not be fair this year. Ask yourself: "Am I being consistent mostly for myself or mostly for my kids?" They need to be able to count on you, and it's best if they can count on a consistent willingness to listen.

Since it's hard enough to be consistent within yourself, it is more than doubly hard to be consistent as a parental couple reacting to rules and consequences and the making of exceptions. There's nothing wrong with an up-front disagreement between you and your spouse over, let's say, whether to give John an extra hour out on Saturday night. Why not let John see each one of you present your case? In the end you will have to reach an agreement, and both of you will have to stick by it. Sticking by it is what's important, so John knows that although you started from different places, you are now together. Letting your kids see your individual differences and the ways you use to work toward a compromise is a beautiful, natural way of getting through.

## FROM PARENT-CHILD TO ADULT-ADULT

Is it human nature for parents always to look upon their children as children, no matter how old they are? Perhaps so, but there is something to be said for the parent who works to put his relationship with his children on a different footing once they reach their late teens. Here is what one father did:

"Once our children got through their secretive periods, around ages fourteen to sixteen, I figured I was all through raising children. I decided I had more to learn from them (since I'd already taught them all that I considered important). So I asked them if they would 'raise' me from then on. At the same time, I told them I felt they had earned their way so far into my heart that I considered them to be among my best friends.

"They said 'yes,' they would be glad to try and raise me from now on, and they considered me one of their best friends. This transition from a parent-child relationship to an adult-adult relationship can be thrilling, and bring a deepening of love no other act could achieve. Of course the original parent-child relationship is not totally dissolved, it is simply on a better footing."

I have watched the children in that family grow into adult life, and I have watched them return to their parents' home and settle into long, open-ended talks with father or mother or both. Every parent is different, and getting through to teenagers is never guaranteed by any formula. But openness, warmth, confidence in oneself and in one's children, together with a keen desire to learn from them as well as to teach them what you know—these four qualities will serve you well. What's more, your children will pick them up and make them a part of their own life style.

## THE PASSAGE OF TIME

If all else fails, parents and teenagers can always count on the curative effect of the passage of time. A conflict waged with hammer and tong this year may seem trifling by next year; the secretive years run their course and communication opens up little by little of its own accord. College, or a job, usually means a separation for most of each year and this makes for many changes, mostly good ones. Consider the perceptiveness of this college student's description of an incident while he was at home during the summer after his freshman year:

"The other night my dad yelled at me because I had gone over to a friend's house and passed out there. I didn't call home, mainly because I would have had a tough time dialing the phone, but also because I didn't want to wake them up at two in the morning to tell them I wasn't coming home until the next day.

"Well, the telephone at my friend's house didn't work for incoming calls, so when my mom called up she couldn't get through and she was frantic. I had just gotten my car the day before and she was sure I had gotten into an accident. My dad was really mad because of what I'd done to my mom. That's a pretty neat attitude on his part. I'm glad he watches out for her as much as he can.

"When I got home the next day, my mom said she was glad to see me. But she didn't tell me she'd been up since five-thirty that morning, driving all over the place trying to track me down. Dad *did* tell me that—which gave me a pretty clear view of the situation, even though it was painful to me because I had such a bad headache."

## TRUST

All of the examples given so far include both love and trust. Trust is an easy word to be cynical about. The saying "trust him no further than you can throw him" dates back to a seventeeth-century English proverb. For many teenagers, it is a greater compliment to be trusted than to be loved.

Trust is not the same as naiveté nor is it the same as neglect. Young children running around town at eleven P.M. on a school night are not trusted, they are neglected. If a teenager suddenly seems to have lots of unaccountable spending money, his parents will be naive, not trusting, if they fail to ask him some questions. Trust implies faith, but like any faith worth having, it also implies appraisal. Trust requires confidence, but real trust is not easily conned.

An eighth-grader stole a ten-speed bicycle and brought it home; he told his father that "a friend gave it to me to keep for a while."

"That's nice," said his ungullible father, "you'll have a chance to see if you really like ten-speeds."

"Yeah."

"What's your friend's name—the one who's letting you keep the bike for him?"

"Jim. You don't know him, he's a friend from school."

"What's Jim's last name?"

"I don't know."

"Where does he live?"

"Somewhere on the other side of school."

"Could you find out his last name tomorrow?"

"I guess so, but what for?"

"I'd just like to know."

The next day, "Jim" suddenly wanted his bike back. The father wondered what the true story might have been, but he let the subject go and he did not stop trusting his son. After all, his son could have been telling the truth and if not, he hoped the boy had learned a lesson the easy way. More important, he knew it is better for parents to be let down once or twice than not to trust their kids at all.

It is sad but true that if you discover that your teenager has lied to you, and if you tell him you can't trust him anymore because of the lie, you are likely to get nothing but more lies. Most of them will be half-truths, actually. Your daughter will say, "I'm going over to Janie's house," and she will go to Janie's house—but she will also rendezvous there with the boy you've told her you don't like. The motives may be trivial, but a cloaked and wordless pattern of deceit has begun, a pattern which will make trust less and less possible for you.

If you ever reach the point where you don't believe anything one of your children says, you lose the ability to use words in communication; you are reduced, literally, to the communication level of animals. Animals communicate by bodily posture, by snarling, by baring teeth, by raising hackles to show anger or by rolling over to show good intentions. Humans will slam doors, pry into closets and drawers, run away from home, take drugs, use their fists or, ultimately, pick up a fatal weapon.

Restoring lost trust is like recovering lost treasure from the bottom of the sea; it is extremely challenging, it requires skill, and it is always worth the effort. To get trust you must give trust. Giving trust is a constant risk. Your gift may be sent back unopened. It may, on the other hand, inspire a similar gift in return.

## SMOTHER LOVE

It is easier to love a teenager than to trust him, and there is a name for love without trust: smother love. It comes in two versions, one too sweet, the other too strict—and it is practiced as commonly by fathers as by mothers.

Have you ever known a kid whose parents think he can do no wrong? He's almost as insufferable as his parents, and no wonder—he has lived on a steady diet of cheap compliments, a diet which, like starch and carbohydrates, will bloat and distort a person. Even worse, he has been cheated out of the glow one feels after being praised by a parent who knows enough to save his congratulations for those rare and deserving moments in life. Unselective praise can hurt a teenager more than all the drugs in your local dealer's kit bag. And the kid who believes his parents' empty words will grow up without learning how to admit his own mistakes, how to lose gracefully, or how to cope with the full force of failure. His parents will be too busy making excuses for him.

At the opposite extreme you have kids who grow up on a short tether, stunted by rigid, unnecessary rules enforced by humorless parents who, down deep, dislike all children, especially their own. Teenagers from families like this become adults who haven't the slightest idea how to handle life's best gift, freedom.

No one enjoys being distrusted. It gnaws deep in the gut. It nags and drains and jades you, and if the people who distrust you are also people who are important to you, the blow can change you permanently. Curiosity fades, life becomes dull, and each day is another day of going through the motions.

Distrust is both the form and the substance of smother love. It is parents who will not give their children the space to grow on their own. It is parents who defend and cover up their children's mistakes by blaming bad friends, bad teachers, bad books. If you ask these parents, "Do you trust your kids?" they will often answer, "Of course we do." But if you ask their kids, they will say, "It doesn't feel that way to us."

Norman is an example of a boy who was never trusted by his parents while he was growing up. It came through to Norman as a lack of confidence, and he dealt with his feeling of inadequacy in a socially acceptable way; he ate a lot. When we met, Norman weighed a doughy two hundred and twenty-five pounds and stood a little under five feet, nine inches tall.

He complained that his parents were nit-pickers, that they never had a kind word for him, that they talked only about his faults. He had taken to faking illness so he could stay home from school, which he called a "bore." The crisis which brought Norman and his family to me was Norman's decision, a decision opposed by both of his parents, to quit school less than halfway through his senior year.

His father is a physically imposing self-made man. When he isn't talking, he seems about to say, "Let's get on with it." He reminded me of Edward G. Robinson in his earlier films, and indeed he possessed some of that actor's gift for drama. He also cared deeply about his son's future and felt certain that dropping out of high school would ruin Norman's chances for a productive life. "But," he explained when we met, "Norman's always been a quitter." During a session with Norman and his parents, I asked his father to explain his feelings about Norman's plan to leave high school and find a job. He began in a low, sincere tone.

"I want you to know that Norman is the most intelligent member of this family. He is more sensitive, more aware, and more concerned than any of the rest of us." He had the silken, assured voice of a Madison Avenue pro doing an insurance commercial.

An edge of sarcasm rimmed his next words. "He knows more than I do, more than his mother, more than his school counselor. Just ask him . . . " His neck swelled tight against his starched collar. ". . . just *ask* him, because he'll tell you himself. He knows it *all.*" His face reddened as he raised his voice for the clincher. "He doesn't need your advice or my advice because he already *knows!* That's why he's failed every one of his classes this quarter, dropped out of school without my permission, and sleeps every day until noon instead of looking for a job—because he's so damned smart!"

Timing, phrasing, innuendo, the slow building of tension and the cathartic, glowering climax—Norman's father had them all. Oration was his strong suit. Norman, nailed to his chair, was mismatched with his father every time, a technical knockout in the first round. Of course Norman is expected to fail. "You're a quitter, Norman; that's all you've ever been, and the way you're going now, that's all you'll ever be." How'd you like to hear that three times a week from your thirteenth to your eighteenth birthdays? It just might make you a quitter.

Norman's parents let him quit school on the condition that he begin a serious search for work. I asked them to lay off the quitter routine, which they did. Even so, I got numerous calls from Norman's mother, all of which had the same message: "Norman never follows through on anything." In tension-filled families there is always a lot of not-following-through. True to form, Norman was turned down by two or three prospective employers and went back to sleeping until noon.

He finally did get a job, and one year later he went back to school. The year had meant something to him, because he had learned how hard life can be without an education. His parents still think he is a quitter, but with some luck he may learn to trust himself enough to make it on his own.

## FIRM LOVE

The opposite of smother love is firm love. I mean firm in three senses: a firm foundation, a firm heart, and a firm hand at the wheel. Dependability, loyalty, trustworthiness. Firm love can be counted on, it is always there no matter what I do. It is resilient, it has muscles that stretch but never break. And it is a hard taskmaster, it always reminds me when I am not giving my best. Most of all, it is love and trust combined.

You may already be using your own variation of firm love, and if you are then you know that it is occasionally strict, occasionally lenient, depending on the circumstances. If you have to tell a twenty-one-year-old son who is still living at home that he must find an apartment of his own, you are using firm love; you don't want him to stunt his own growth by staying too long in the nest. When you ask him to leave, you are following a law so basic that it is understood by every animal in the kingdom, large or small, but that doesn't mean the words come easily. Firm love will often test your resolve and tempt you to smother.

Allowing your teenager to attend an unchaperoned party can also be firm love. To begin with, it demonstrates your trust. Trust inspires loyalty in return. A teenager is more likely to get into trouble when he feels he is not trusted. If you are worried about the unchaperoned party, ask yourself why. Because the kids there might use drugs? Sneak into the bedrooms? Comport themselves in unseemly ways? Use foul language? If the actual party does include all of these improprieties, do you envision your teenager as instigator, participant, or bystander? If the latter, do you trust him to form his own conclusions? If not, or if your vision focuses on one of the first two possibilities, then you know you need a long talk with your teenager. Nothing erodes a good parent-teenager relationship as quickly as the drip-drip-dripping of distrust.

Now let's turn the coin over again, because firm love can be as relentless as a prosecutor in a courtroom. If you are running a business and discover that you have an alcoholic employee, the worst thing you can do is confront him with your suspicions. If you say, "Joe, I think you're drinking too much," Joe will deny it and blame everyone but himself. He will say, "Who told you I drink too much? My wife? Well, she hates me anyway. I should've divorced her a long time ago. Or maybe it was Harry that told you? You know he's always been jealous of me because he's after my job."

If you want to get through to Joe, you've got to come to him with the facts. You've got to say, "Joe, you've missed three Fridays and two Monday in the past month. You're missing from your desk periodically during the afternoons. The market survey you ran this month was a week late. Last month it was three days late." You come to Joe with the facts, and you tell him that he can't keep his job unless he gets help, and that if he gets help he will have a good chance of getting well. You give him plenty of time to improve, but you tell him that you're going to meet regularly with him to check his progress. A parent can use exactly the same strategy with a teenager on the downslide.

When she was fourteen, Tracy had a brief romance with a college student and got pregnant. She had a miscarriage, the boy disappeared, and she buried her hurt so deeply inside herself that she was able to pretend it was gone. But it wasn't really gone, and she began nipping on her father's bourbon, skipping school, failing to do her chores at home, and abusing her curfew. A counselor at school caught her drinking in the girls' room. She started spending time with a rowdy bunch.

Tracy's parents met with the school counselor and together they decided to gather some evidence: days and hours missing from school, grades dropping from B's to F's, inches of bourbon sneaked, lies told, and money taken from mother's purse. They spent a month taking notes, and then they all sat down for a talk that pulled Tracy up short and turned her around.

If you have ever had to listen to a bill of particulars against yourself, you can imagine how burned up Tracy was that day. When her parents started citing the evidence, her first boiling reaction was "You've been spying on me!" Her parents were as gentle as possible, but they wanted her to hear it all, to hear what her life sounded like when it was condensed into a month's worth of deceit. Tracy lapsed into a long silence, but she was grudgingly impressed with her parents' thoroughness; as far as she knew, they hadn't missed a thing. Much later she remembered thinking, "If they've gone to all this trouble, they must really care about me."

At the end of the discussion Tracy's parents did not say, "We'd appreciate it if you would go talk to a counselor." They said, "We are going to call a counselor we know *right now* and make an appointment. If he wants to see all of us, we'll go too."

Confrontation is the child of true caring. From a teenager's point of view, there is a thin line between nosiness and caring, a line that too many parents are all too willing to cross. We need to work to respect that line. We also need to bring kids like Tracy face to face with their own self-destructive behavior because to do so is to demonstrate firm love at its best.

Many parents have found that the main problem they have is not that they can't communicate, but that they communicate only too well: they understand their kids perfectly and disagree with them totally. At bottom, it is a basic difference of opinion about what is right and what is wrong.

# 4

## Ethics

The big question behind what is right and wrong is how people *decide* what is right and wrong. Teenagers are often excellent attorneys for their own defense. If you think a particular act was wrong but your son thinks it was, at worst, neither wrong nor right, how do the two of you make your way to common ground? You can start by trying to discover which of the three most common moral philosophies is the one you use as the starting point for your moral decisions.

The first is code ethics. Several thousand years of human history have left us with standards, laws, wise sayings—the makings of a moral plan. Your decisions about right and wrong, if based on code ethics, are thus founded on a combination of law and folk wisdom. For many people the code includes everything from the Ten Commandments to Aunt Lila's homespun aphorisms.

The second is situation ethics. No absolute right or wrong exists here except for the absolute rightness of using love—preferably selfless love—as a moral compass. Every moral decision you make depends on the unique circumstances and the personalities involved in the situation.

The third has been summed up in a hip phrase, "Do your own thing." It is a loose form of existentialism: you do what you want, you stay in the moment, and you make every moment count. Nothing is wrong unless it is your failure to face life honestly and to live it as you see fit. Your moral decisions are spontaneous, unprincipled (because you accept no universal laws or principles), and unpredictable.

To test these three moral philosophies, I offer ten actual cases, each one presenting a specific moral dilemma commonly faced by parents and children. Read them over now, and in the closing pages of this chapter we'll see if it is possible to settle the issues raised in each case.

### Case 1. Turn the other cheek?

Mr. Smith's eight-year-old son came home from school crying. One of the other boys had punched him hard, right in the nose, but he hadn't fought back. His Sunday School teacher had given a lesson only the week before on Jesus' saying, "Turn the other cheek."

Mr. Smith comforted his son and wondered at the wisdom of that saying. Should he tell his son to fight back next time?

### Case 2. Beer before truth?

The kids are organizing a giant mid-summer keg party in the woods behind Jones's abandoned farm. From two hundred and fifty to four hundred kids are sure to be there; it's the big event of the summer. Dave, age sixteen, plans to go.

"Bye, Mom," he says as he starts out the door.

"Where will you be tonight?"

"Oh, Fred and Jim and me will probably go to a show at the drive-in, so don't expect me until late."

"Okay. Just be careful on the road."

Should Dave have told his mother the truth?

### Case 3. Steal from the profit kings?

Henry shoplifts from large department stores. He has never been caught. Since his fourteenth birthday he has taken hundreds of dollars' worth of clothes, records, tapes, books, and art supplies. He rationalizes it like this:

"Those big stores rip people off every day with their high prices, so I'm just making the score a little more even."

He talks about all the other people who do what he does, including housewives stealing food from grocery stores. Is his stealing justified?

### Case 4. Lying for love.

Julie, a high school senior, has been going steady with Bob for two years. Her parents come home one evening to find her alone with Bob in the basement family room. They ask her to come upstairs and send Bob home. Later they claim that she took "an unusually long time" to come up the steps and that her clothes appeared wrinkled. They forbid her to see Bob again.

Julie is furious. She insists that she and Bob were doing "nothing wrong." In fact, Julie is a virgin and plans to stay that way until the day she marries Bob.

She begins lying to her parents about her weekend plans so she can see Bob on the sly. Is she wrong to do this?

### Case 5. Withholding the truth.

Mary, eighteen, is pregnant. A talented art major at the state university, she's excited about her future. She loves her boyfriend, John, and they plan to marry and have children—but not for several more years.

"We want children," Mary says, "but we want to have them when we're prepared to give them a good life." Mary is afraid to talk with her parents. She and John empty their savings and Mary makes plans to get an abortion.

"I just couldn't tell my parents about this," she says. "Especially not my dad. He loves me so much that it would break his heart, and I know he'd forgive me in the end, but he'd never forgive John." Is Mary right to keep the secret and have an abortion?

### Case 6. Politeness versus self-expression.

Mimi is seventy-eight. She loves to have her grandchildren to dinner but she considers them a thoughtless lot. They show up wearing faded jeans, old shirts, and occasionally no shoes. Mimi is accustomed to more formal or at least more appropriate attire. Her evening meals are attended by a servant who looks after her. He's important to her and she worries that he will feel insulted by the casual dress of her grandchildren.

The kids, who actually have excellent manners despite their ragged appearance, feel that Mimi, along with other adults, should accept them the way they are. Two of the girls scarcely even own dresses anymore.

Would Mimi be wrong to insist that the kids wear ties or dresses when they come to dinner at her house?

### Case 7. The right to privacy?

Cindy, age fourteen, is enjoying her secretive years. She says very little when she's around the house. Her mother believes that "any parent with a fourteen-year-old daughter should search her room at least once a week." So Cindy's drawers are checked, her mail is read, and her phone calls are monitored.

When Cindy protested, her mother said, "If I could trust you to tell me the truth, I wouldn't have to look through your things, but you don't say anything around here anymore." Cindy ran away from home, talked with a counselor, and insisted that the one condition of her return home be a guarantee of privacy. Was Cindy right to protest?

### Case 8. Conscience versus obedience.

Larry, seventeen, disagrees with the current administration in Washington. His father is an ardent and thoughtful supporter of the incumbent president. A demonstration against administration policies is planned on the campus of a nearby university, and Larry wants to go.

His father flatly refuses to let him take part in the demonstration. He feels that Larry has failed to think through all the issues. Larry insists that he has a right to express his own views, and walks out of the house in defiance of his father's orders. Is he right to attend the demonstration?

### Case 9. Turn in your own daughter?

Mrs. Young has little faith in counseling agencies. Her daughter, Sarah, hangs around with "the worst kind" of kids. Sarah is sixteen; she has run away from home four times, and she has a twenty-one-year-old boyfriend who has already had a paternity suit filed against him by the parents of another girl. The local police tell Mrs. Young that several of Sarah's best friends are known opium dealers.

"Sarah lies about everything," her mother says. "She is such a good manipulator that she has everyone under her thumb, including *my* psychiatrist!"

Mrs. Young must choose between turning Sarah over to juvenile authorities, who plan to send her to a state home-school for at least a year, or allowing her to join a local therapy group and continue living at home. She doesn't want to see her daughter go to an institution, but she fears Sarah will use the therapy group to reinforce her own rebellious acts. What should Mrs. Young do?

### Case 10. Turn in your own father?

Linda's father is a secret alcoholic. Her mother walked out on the family, saying she never wanted to see any of them again. Linda is seventeen; her only brother, Tim, is nine. She watches her father get drunk every night and, when she tries to stop him, he slaps her. If Tim acts up while his father is drinking, he is severely beaten.

Linda is afraid to act. Her father is a well-respected business executive. Yet she feels that life with her father is unbearable and worries about what will happen to Tim when she has graduated and moved into a place of her own.

Should Linda "turn her father in" by calling child welfare?

## DO WHAT YOU WANT

The loosest answer to all ten of these cases is to instruct everyone to do whatever he feels like doing. And what a person feels like doing might be selfish or generous, sacrificial or hedonistic, all depending on the person. In fact, the same person could easily display all of those stripes in the space of a few days, as indeed most of us humans do.

The person who eschews all moral laws is not always automatically immoral. He may actually lead a more virtuous life than the person who governs all decisions by strict moral codes. Jesus himself fought against many of the outdated laws of his time and tried to return people to a simpler morality in which one loved his God with all his heart, and his neighbor as himself.

Jesus' emphasis on this point gave birth, perhaps unwittingly, to a group of people who believed that faith alone, not obedience to the law, is the path to salvation. They were lawless people but they were not immoral; in a sense, their beliefs were based on the new "code" which Jesus had taught. Today we have a new breed of freethinking people who subscribe to no particular moral laws. If your mind's eye conjures up an image of wine-glutted hedonists and long-hairs preaching "do your own thing," you have only half the picture. There are many other freethinking folks who are simple, kind, and gentle folk with no axes to grind.

If we all decided to be freethinkers, the world would surely collapse. But the rebels do provide a good leaven in society's lump. They are a nonjudgmental lot because many of them have indulged themselves without guilt in an extensive catalogue of what a Baptist would call sins. But if prudent followers of the code all had one such friend, a person to whom we could unburden our souls and who would judge us not, the psychologists would lose most of their business.

## CODE ETHICS

If the freethinkers are the leaven, the stern visage of John Calvin is the lump. There will be no take-over of society as long as Calvin's shadow falls, as it does even today, from Maine to the eastern border of California.

Right and wrong are rarely in doubt when you travel in code ethics country. There is a rule for every form of human behavior and a couple of rules standing by for the vices nobody has thought of yet. A judge has estimated that we now have more than twenty-five million laws on the books, all passed to enforce the ten commandments.

With people adding to the code every year, it is no wonder that different parts of it contradict each other. We say "Do not kill" and we condemn promiscuity, but we also say, "All's fair in love and war." Both statements are part of the code. So is "Turn the other cheek," a teaching that few individuals and no nations have ever taken seriously.

Sex outside of marriage is wrong because "good people have always thought so," and many Christians and Jews believe that the Bible supports this point of view.* Another common view is that couples who marry and decide to have no children are verging on immorality because they have obviously married just for sex.

Most parents gravitate toward code ethics, and this becomes the razor's edge of parent-teenager arguments because most young people rebel against at least some part of the code. This rebellion is a natural and necessary life process, and most rebels return eventually to the main tenets of the code. The old laws have much to recom-

---

* The Bible is actually less than clear about sex. Betrothed couples were allowed to have sexual relations in biblical times. The Old Testament celebrates the institution of marriage, but King David purchased his wife Michal for the price of 100 Philistine foreskins; he also paid scant attention to the fact that Michal was married to another man. We are told in the New Testament that if we marry a divorced woman we are automatically guilty of adultery unless her former husband is dead; and according to Paul, we are on our best behavior if we simply avoid touching a member of the opposite sex altogether.

mend them and don't seem so stuffy once they have been ground down a bit on the honing stones of one's personal experience.

The underlying spirit of code ethics is violated by two types of people—those who reject the laws entirely and those who obey the laws slavishly. People who dislike the code may turn into lifelong freethinkers, but most of the holdouts settle on a way of deciding right and wrong which marches these days under the banner of

## SITUATION ETHICS

Its critics think that situation ethics is easy—a cheaply disguised version of lawlessness, a devil in an angel's gown. Nevertheless, a true believer in this type of ethic has actually chosen the most difficult method for making moral decisions. (Code ethics is the easiest because it leaves so little to doubt.) When you follow a situation ethic, you make love the guiding norm for your every decision; the comfort of knowing in advance what is right and what is wrong is back in code country.

Joseph Fletcher, an Episcopal theologian, is one of the main apologists for situation ethics. He cites a scene from Richard Nash's play *The Rainmaker* to illustrate the essence of the moral decision-making process. In the film version of the play, Burt Lancaster plays Starbuck, an itinerant con man who comes to a ranch in the midwest during a drought and promises to bring rain. Katharine Hepburn plays Lizzie, the rancher's daughter who fears life is passing her by, and her younger brother Noah fuels her fear by calling her an old maid.

Starbuck's winning spirit is like a fresh breeze in the dusty homestead, and Lizzie begins to hope again. Toward the end of the play she joins Starbuck in the stable tack room where he always spends the night. Her father has watched her go and he is content to let it be, but Noah is appalled. "It ain't right, Pop, it ain't right!" he shouts, grabbing a rifle so he can go out and rescue Lizzie from Starbuck and from herself. His father explodes:

"Noah, you're so full of what's right you can't see what's good!" He knows as any father would that Lizzie may always be an old maid, but he says, "She's gotta have somethin'! *Lizzie has got to have somethin'!* Even if it's only one minute—with a man talkin' quiet and his hand touchin' her face."

There is sometimes a difference between what's right and what's good; that is the essential vision of situation ethics. What happens in the tack room between Lizzie and Starbuck may not be right according to the code, but it might be good in human terms. It may give them both something—a shared moment of love—even if that moment survives only as a memory.

The weakness of situation ethics is the wisdom it requires. Few of us have lived long and deeply enough to bring to each and every moral decision the necessary credentials: experience, patience, empathy, and an abiding love for people. Lizzie's father had all of those qualities, but he is perhaps a rare person.

## RESPONSIBILITY

Parents love this word. What they usually mean by it is "duty." Mowing the lawn is Jack's responsibility (duty); being home by midnight is Jane's responsibility (duty). This is a one-dimensional use of the word.

Richard Niebuhr, the late professor of Christian ethics at Yale, believed that the central meaning of responsibility can be found in its root word—response. We cannot talk about responsibility without also talking about how we respond to other people, people who count on us. The questions are: to whom am I responsible, for what, and for how long?

It is our right to go where we please, but it is our duty to stop at a red light and to drive on the right side of the road; if we didn't do this, society would collapse. These are examples of *mere* responsibility, those actions required of all of us to help keep the world in one piece. We must never fail to do less than uphold our mere responsibilities.

Around the house, family members also have certain rights and certain duties. It is Jack's right to have an allowance simply because he is a member of the family. It is his duty to cut the grass, not to earn money but to make his fair contribution to family life. Keeping the lawn trimmed and neat is his mere responsibility; it is the least he can do.

*Moral* responsibility goes a step further. It means Jack should not cut off the cat's tail in his haste to finish the lawn. It means loving your children in addition to giving them food, clothing, shelter, and an education. We have the time and energy to be morally responsible to only a few people during one lifetime. Moral responsibility implies much more than an automatic reaction, much more than stopping when the light is red.

A moral response is a risk taken. When I respond to another person (rather than simply reacting to him), I take the chance that I may be changed by what he says and does. I have my own opinion, but I am open to his opinion. Because of this, a moral response is always an act of trust.

Some moral decisions are clear-cut. Others seem complicated when we are trying to make them and simple when, a year later, we look back at them. And still others remain complex for all time. We do not always have the luxury of choosing between an obvious right and an obvious wrong; we often must choose instead between two actions which both seem equally wrong or equally right. Here is an example:

### Case 11. Call home or wait until morning?

Jo, sixteen, has just shown up at my drop-in center. She has been on the run for two days and she wants a place to sleep for a few nights. She knows I have access to a number of private families who have volunteered to take in runaways on a temporary basis.

"Have you talked with your parents since you left home?"

"No."

"Do you want to?"

"No."

"Not even a call to let them know you're safe?"

"*No.* I don't want to talk to them yet, I'm not ready. My mom would just cry and make me feel terrible. I need a little more time to think."

"What if I called them, anonymously, just to say you're safe and you'll be in touch when you're ready?"

"No. When the time comes, I want to make the call myself."

A real conversation wouldn't be that condensed because a counselor would space his suggestions about phoning over an hour's worth of talking, but most runaways are like Jo—they don't want to talk to their parents right away. As a counselor, I know what her parents are going through, I know that any call will be a partial relief, and I also know that Jo is already regarding me with suspicion. If she decides to walk out the door, I have no authority to hold her against her will and I will have lost whatever chance I have to work on getting her home again. What should I do?

In many states I am required by law to call Jo's parents even at the risk of losing her to the streets. Some counselors bend the law for a few hours to give themselves time to build trust, but the code does provide a clear mandate: if I can't persuade Jo to call, I am obligated to call her parents myself, immediately.

Quite apart from what the law says, what would be the best thing to do in this situation? I could make a compromise with Jo, give her a place to stay on the condition that first thing in the morning we talk over what has happened and end our talk with a call to her home. This would give me more time to build a trusting relationship between Jo and myself, but it will also subject her parents to another anxious night. The best therapy for Jo might be to insist that she face and fulfill her moral responsibility to ease her parents' fears by dialing a phone. The question remains: what course do I take?

Counselors respond to this common dilemma in many different ways and styles. I give it to you in order to emphasize the complexity of many moral problems, the shades of gray that often make a decision difficult. In Jo's case, it is right to call her parents *and* it is right to give her time to collect her thoughts.


## VALUE CLARIFICATION

Every serious dispute between parents and teenagers is rooted in values. The arguments rarely get far because most parents use the code to support their points while most young people are likely to use a street-modified version of situation ethics. It is like a pro football game in which the parents' team is playing by NFL rules and the kids' team by Canadian rules.

The exercise outlined on the next few pages won't declare a winner, but it will help you clarify what is really at stake. I have listed fifteen qualities or behavior patterns that I'm guessing you might like to see in your teenagers. Look them over and then rate them, giving a "1" to the quality you value most highly on through to a "15" for the one which is least important to you. Keep in mind that these are qualities which you appreciate or want to encourage in your teenager, though they may also be values you prize for yourself.

Then, in a parenthesis next to your first rating, put a second number, a number to represent the order in which you believe your teenager would rank the same item. For example, if you rank appearance first but you think that your teenager would rank it tenth, your ratings would look like this:

1 (10) Appearance: clothes, hair, etc.

You can do this exercise alone if you wish, but you'll learn more by getting your whole family together so you can compare reactions. If one of your kids does the exercise, have him rate each quality first for himself and then, in parenthesis, in the order he believes you would choose.

> Appearance: clothes, hair, etc.
> Abstinence from drugs, including alcohol
> Attendance at church
> Curiosity
> Choice of friends
> Freedom
> Independence
> Initiative
> Neatness
> Open-mindedness
> Performance in school: grades
> Sticking to the rules at home and elsewhere
> Telling the truth
> Time spent at home with the family
> Virginity

Now go back over the list and indicate, to the right of each item, how often it is discussed or debated in your family. If the neatness of everyone's room is the most frequently discussed subject on the list, it should get a "1"; if curiosity is never discussed, you should give it a "15."

Families usually have a lot of fun comparing notes after doing this exercise. What surprises you about the order in which another family member has ranked each item? Are there any big differences between what you thought someone else valued and what that person actually thinks is important? Do you and your spouse have significant differences? Is there an item that everyone values highly but is rarely discussed? If there is, don't assume this is a bad sign—freedom might be highly rated by everyone and also be such a natural part of your family's daily life that it doesn't need to be talked about in so many words.

If you have rated telling the truth, abstinence from drugs, and performance in school very highly—and you spend most of your time arguing about hair length, faded jeans, and sloppy rooms—then you know you're wasting most of your ammunition on small game. And how did everyone rate the risky, growth-producing values—curiosity, independence, initiative, and open-mindedness? Teenagers often put these near the top of their list while parents tend to put them in the middle. If you followed this tendency, take heed. Your middle choices are the ones you have the least feeling about, one way or the other. The most revealing ratings are your first four and your last four.

## ANALYSIS OF THE CASES

Now let's return to the cases which began this chapter. Remember that what follows is my own analysis; *every* conclusion is arguable. The main reason for looking at each case in detail is to get some practice in the art of making moral choices because each case did happen in real life and an actual decision had to be made by the people involved.

Mr. Smith *(Case One)*, whose small boy was punched in the nose, is a professor at a large eastern university. He visited a colleague whose specialty was ethics and explained the dilemma: should a small boy always turn the other cheek? The ethics professor said, "Tell your boy to hit back. He is still too young to know the difference between prudence and cowardice."

That reply demonstrates situation ethics at its best. The moral solution depended on the particular circumstances of the case, specifically the age and experience of Mr. Smith's boy. Some day he will be old enough to know the difference between prudence and cowardice, and on that day he will have to make a fresh decision about what is best.

Although "turn the other cheek" is part of the code, so is "an eye for an eye and a tooth for a tooth." Jesus intended to set that Old Testament saying aside, but most of mankind has tended to side with Dryden's observation that "self-defense is nature's eldest law."

Dave *(Case Two)* should have told his mother the truth, according to the code. To begin with, he is up against the fifth commandment, "Honor thy father and thy mother." The Old Testament is very specific about what "honor" means: children of *any* age must not curse, strike, disgrace or despise their parents. Parents are to be submitted to and obeyed. Another part of the code comes from modern law: Dave is a minor and drinking beer is, in his case, against the law.

Dave knows this, of course, so he lies to his mother both to get himself out of the house and to keep her from feeling any obligation to report what she knows to the police. The keg party is really a game; the object is to drink as much beer as possible before some adult finds out and reports it to the police. When the police come, the object is to get away and arrive home safely with a good alibi. As long as parents, police, and teenagers play this game, the rules will never vary; Dave will always lie to his parents because he knows they will make him stay home if he tells the truth.

Teenagers who are basically honest will lie to their parents when they believe they have no other choice. If Dave's parents had told him at some earlier point that they knew keg parties were a custom, that they assumed he went to them now and then, and that they wanted to know the next time he planned to go to one, he might have told them the truth. In that event, they could ask him several pertinent questions:

First, will the party disturb people in nearby homes? Second, could you be arrested? Third, could any other serious harm come to you or to other kids at the party? Might someone with too much to drink have an accident on the way home?

Dave could answer truthfully: no, the party will be very isolated; yes, if the police come they will stop the party, pour out the beer, and try to catch the celebrants—although they are never fast enough to succeed; and yes, some kind may try to drive when he's loaded—people do it every day. But Dave assures his parents he would not try to drive if he were drunk.

If you were Dave's parents, you would have to rationalize if you wanted to give him permission to go. I mean rationalize in the best sense of that word—"to make conformable to reason." Is it reasonable to say that it is not your job as a parent to wipe out every foolish act committed by your children, that some antics are not worth the energy required to combat them? Most policemen allow people to drive a few miles above the speed limit. A parent must watch his children's behavior and correct serious skullduggery; he must also distinguish between real felonies and minor infractions. It is not his duty to correct his child's every fault, partly because that job is impossible, but mostly because if he tries, he will never have time for anything else.

Respect for property *(Case Three)* is at an all-time low in this country. Some of the most circumspect young people, kids who are honest in every other respect, see nothing wrong with stealing a steak from a grocery store or a pocket radio from a department store. When Henry points to all the other people who steal from the big stores, he is not exaggerating.

A Harvard survey asked a wide sampling of children, "Do you think men who run large companies are honest?" If they were eleven years or older, they answered "no" in resounding majorities. But this does not get at the moral right and wrong of stealing; it is merely one man's frustrated search for a reason why we are having so much of it today.

The code speaks clearly enough in Henry's case. "Thou shalt not steal" is an old moral law, and it is echoed in every city's statutes. Even when Henry tries to justify his actions by pointing a finger at price-gouging merchants, the code answers him with an old bit of folk wisdom, "Two wrongs don't make a right."

But the code is being ignored these days. In most cities theft has reached epidemic proportions and the thieves are often young people, not only ghetto kids, but rich kids as well. High prices, advertising, and the lure of instant gratification have written a new law for a large minority of today's youth: "Take what you can get." This way of thinking will never be counteracted by juvenile detention centers where new rip-off techniques are traded like bubblegum cards. Perhaps, instead, the young may eventually convert the young back to an old and honorable value: earning.

Julie *(Case Four)* is caught between two undesirable choices. She can stop seeing Bob, as her parents have demanded; or she can lie to them, as in fact she did, in order to see Bob secretly. She plans to marry Bob some day and does not want to break off their relationship. But Julie is an extremely moral person, a strong believer in the importance of respecting one's parents, so her decision to deceive them was not an easy one.

The code appears to stand against Julie since she certainly does not honor her parents by lying to them. If you are a believer in situation ethics you might ask her, "What will be the consequences if your parents discover that you are still seeing Bob?" And most important, "What effect will the weeks and months of deception have on *you?*" If Julie insists that her love for Bob is strong enough both to require deception and to endure it, then she will have made the best of a bad situation.

The real Julie became so upset about the secret nature of her relationship with Bob that she began to resent both Bob and her parents. She forced herself through a reappraisal of her feelings about Bob. "Do I love him so much that I am willing to hurt my parents? If lying to them is going to ruin us as a couple anyway, what's the point of going on?" In the end, she petitioned her parents for a reconsideration of her right to see Bob. They did not give in until they saw the strength of her will and, possibly, a hint of her pain. It was a hard decision for Julie, but on the day she made it she crossed the borderline between adolescence and maturity.

When Mary found out she was pregnant *(Case Five)*, she had to face two moral problems. First, should she tell her parents? Second, should she have the baby?

Her gut feeling was "I don't want my parents to know." Her fear of their disapproval was more powerful than any of her other emotions. She was convinced that she would lose their respect and that her boyfriend, John, would bear the brunt of the blame for her pregnancy. Mary thus decided in favor of another old folk saying, "Some truths are better left untold."

Once she had made the decision to keep her pregnancy secret, she had no choice but to get an abortion. It may be that most people in our society believe abortion is wrong, particularly in Mary's case: she was not a victim of rape and there was no reason to believe her baby would be unhealthy. But legally she had every right to seek an abortion; in that sense, the code was on her side. Morally, a growing number of people have concluded that Mary's decision is such an intensely personal one that it is not our place to judge the rightness or wrongness of what she does, at least not in the early months of her pregnancy.

Mary never regretted her decision. She and John are married today and plan to begin a family soon. Mary may have been right when she kept her crisis from her parents, although she will never know for sure. Teenage girls often underestimate their parents' ability to respond with love, understanding, and concrete help in a time of serious trouble.

Sacrifice is a natural part of family life. Mimi has her standards *(Case Six)* and her grandchildren have theirs. If they are to enjoy one another's company, one side or the other will have to make a sacrifice. The kids will either have to dress up a bit or Mimi will have to dress her dinners down.

Jonathan Weiss, a lawyer and the son of Yale philosopher Paul Weiss, once asked his father the following question: "Which should we applaud more—a swimmer who is fast or a swimmer who is beautiful? In the old days Yale had three great swimmers: Marshall,

MacLean, and Moore. Moore was letter perfect; MacLean was very, very elegant; Marshall splashed like mad. But basically they interchanged the championships. If the function of a sport is in part to supply a spectacle, should we not approve most of Moore?"

His father replied that swimmers should get prizes for gracefulness as well as for speed. The fact that we award only the winner, the first man to touch the finish line, merely shows how obsessed we are by our nation's emphasis on winning.

Mimi's grandchildren might win their point—that they have a right to dress as they please and that adults should accept them for what they are; however, they would be more graceful if they dressed up to go to Mimi's house. The point is not always to win, but to live with a certain amount of grace.

Mimi's dilemma is also faced by parents who want their blue-jeaned sons and daughters to "dress up" for company. A child does have obligations to his family and it would be selfish and imprudent for a teenager to refuse to dress up at his parents' request for some special occasion. It would be equally imprudent and a misuse of power for parents to make such a request *repeatedly* when they know their children hate to do it.

The code sides with Cindy *(Case Seven)* and with Linda *(Case Ten)*. Children must honor their parents, but the fifth commandment also implies that parents should deal properly with their children. Parents should not "provoke their children to anger" nor should they unnecessarily discourage their children (Ephesians 6:4; Colossians 3:21). Cindy's mother both angered and discouraged her with obsessive violations of her privacy. Cindy didn't help matters by running away, but when we look at the situation through her eyes, it's hard to see what other choice she had.

In Linda's family, the dominant note had become injury. Her father's alcoholism was destroying everyone. Loyalty is a central quality in every healthy family. In Linda's case, loyalty demands that she seek help for her brother, her father, and herself. Linda did talk with a caseworker at the welfare department shortly after she graduated from high school, and her brother was placed in a foster home.

Loyalty is also the issue for Larry *(Case Eight)*. He is caught in a tension felt by many devoted family members: the pull between loyalty to a parent and loyalty to the greater world into which we must grow. The political rally is part of that world and Larry's attendance is his only way of expressing his concern.

In order to grow, a young person must try new ideas. If we are both strict and fair, we must say that Larry should obey his father's command, but that his father should not have ordered him to stay home from the rally. This position recognizes Larry's debt to the family which has supported him throughout his life. It also recognizes the truth that parents should not prevent their children from exploring the world in which they live. Unfortunately it also solves nothing: we still have Larry going to the rally in open defiance of his father's orders.

We should ask, "Is Larry's father a politician or a public figure who might be hurt or seriously embarrassed by his son's appearance at the rally?" If Larry's action could harm his father's career, he should think more carefully before making up his mind to go; just how important is this rally? But assuming that Larry can't hurt his father's career by going to the rally, his father might have offered a simple compromise. Larry could attend the rally on the condition that he read a book, chosen by his father, presenting another political viewpoint. Then, together, they could discuss both the rally and the book.

Mrs. Young *(Case Nine)* is not a trusting person. She distrusts her daughter, all counselors, and apparently her own psychiatrist. Since Sarah has run away four times, the court authorities know that she needs special treatment. Their own evaluation has led them to believe that Sarah should be sent to a county-home school, which means they have already ruled out two less drastic alternatives: outpatient counseling and a foster home.

Though it may seem harsh, Mrs. Young will serve her daughter best by agreeing with the court. Keeping mother and daughter under the same roof might succeed only in destroying them both.

A mother of four remembers her mother telling her: "You were fine until you turned sixteen." It was at sixteen that she had stopped cleaning her room.

Children enter their teens echoing their parents' values. They will defend with passion the habits, tastes, and political preferences of their parents. This is the age when people say, "He's his father's son!" and "Isn't she pretty—so much like her mother!"

Then a border is crossed and a time of questioning begins. Perhaps half of all teenagers reject their parents' values entirely. They go through a lawless, experimental period during which anything new is worth one try. Some of these kids are obvious rebels because they are so vocal. Others are quiet and diplomatic around the house but, once outside, they are just as irrepressible as their more vocal confederates.

These young people emerge from their experimental years with a healthy down payment on their own values. They have opinions and priorities which are new, which their parents do not share— even though many of their habits and beliefs have obvious roots in the personalities of their parents: a fastidiousness learned from mother, a slow-to-anger trait from father, or a regard for personal loyalty inherited from them both.

Actually this describes only half of all teenagers, the half who get their rebellion in early and make it stick. The other half includes kids who feel no need to rebel and kids who are suppressed either by their parents or by their own insecurity. A few kids in each category will come out of the closet as adults and, feeling a need for the fun and independence they missed when they were younger, they will rebel against husbands, wives, or jobs. Another much smaller group of young people go into their experimental years and make them a permanent way of life. They become either the most creative geniuses or the most obnoxious drunks in our society, and occasionally they play both those roles with equal distinction.

The experimental years are hard on everyone, parents included. One mother coined her frustration when she said, "I wish we could bury 'em when they're thirteen and dig 'em back up when they're seventeen!" An alternative to that is to step back and look at the whole process—the echoing of parental values during the pre-teenage years, then the questioning, rejecting, experimenting, and finally the partial return. It is a vital, risky, and necessary pilgrimage toward maturity. Liberal parents must never sponsor their children's rebellion, and conservative parents must resist their temptation to squelch it.

In *Cat's Cradle*, Kurt Vonnegut, Jr., describes a bored and lonely God who creates the earth and then decides to make living creatures out of the mud so the mud can see what He has done. The last of God's creatures was man, and man was the only one who could speak—so God leaned close as man sat up, looked around, and spoke. Man blinked.

"What is the purpose of all this?" man asked politely.

"Everything must have a purpose?" asked God.

"Certainly," said man.

"Then I leave it to you to think of one for all this," said God. And then He went away.

Young people are like Vonnegut's first man. They turn thirteen, sit up, look around, and ask, "What is the purpose of all this?" And when they do, we are best advised to resist the speeches and sermons that come so easily to mind. Instead we should give them a reliable compass, a lot of love, and our promise of a fire in the hearth whenever they need it.

# 5

## Discipline

I was caught red-handed walking out of the grocery store with a Milky Way clutched in my pocket. It was a burning, blue day in Los Alamos, New Mexico, and I was eight years old. An alert assistant manager had turned my candy-bar heist into a bust. One hour later my mother came to pick me up; it had taken the manager half that time just to pump my name out of me.

On the way home my mother was silent. She stared ahead at the road and gripped the wheel of our '48 Pontiac. I was her first child and her only son, and she made no effort to wipe away the quiet tears that wet her face before we pulled into the driveway.

I can remember her asking a question then, something like "Don't we give you enough allowance?" And I must have reassured her that a quarter was really more than ample for my needs since the Saturday afternoon movie was only a dime and the box of popcorn a nickel. No, I didn't need more money.

Anger never became part of that experience. Only my mother's sadness. Nothing was said of it ever again, and in the weeks that followed I made friends with the store manager, a lean, dour man who understood my need for atonement. I wasn't punished for what I had done, at least not in the traditional sense. I didn't have to go to my room, endure a lecture, or be spanked. My crime was too overwhelming for such pedestrian tactics. But I haven't stolen a thing since then. Sitting in the front seat watching my mother cry—cry because of *me*—was the most effective "discipline" I ever received.

Most parents feel confident enough about discipline procedures while their children are still small, but confidence doesn't always inspire intelligence. The other day I watched a young, obviously frustrated mother spank the salt out of her three-year-old son while they were standing at the grocery store meat counter. Then she dragged him the length of the store to an exit as he howled and she shouted, "I won't be in a public place with you acting like this!" His crime had been to dawdle along behind her, fingering miscellaneous items on the shelves.

Now that kid may be a certified brat, or his mother may have been having a difficult day, and one humiliation in a grocery store won't scar the kid for life. On the other hand, little kids grow up to be big kids and ten years from now that little boy will be thirteen, and he will be capable of serious mutiny. He will be armed with a thousand "but's" and reasons why and, at times, a what-are-you-going-to-do-about-it attitude. He will certainly be too old to spank and drag the length of the grocery store aisles.

So what do you do? If you share anything in common with most parents of teenagers, you will fall back on the old go-to-your-room technique, which nowadays is called

## GROUNDING

Whenever your teenager breaks an established rule, begin by asking yourself, "Do I want to punish him because I'm so mad at him regardless of whether it does any good? Or do I want to change his behavior too?" Most kids do not change as a result of their parents' discipline; they are inconvenienced now and then by what you do, but not changed. For many kids, grounding is a good example of a punishment which inconveniences but seldom changes the way they behave. In fact it may even be a pleasant change of pace.

"Grounding never upset me," says a young man who is now in college. "I was between twelve and fourteen when my parents were using it. I was running with a small group of friends and I wasn't going to parties or out on dates. So grounding wasn't really cramping my style that much; I'd just figure out things to do around the house. I'd read books, clean up my room, write, do something constructive."

Of course most teenagers do hate to be grounded. Even the

person I've just quoted would have felt its impact if his parents had used it at a time when it *would* have cramped his style. Even though you do want a discipline technique to make an impression, you don't want it to backfire. Leslie, fifteen, expressed her feelings succinctly: "Being grounded drives me up the wall." The most important element in her life is her time with her friends. She likes books too, but she'd rather read them in the company of other people, preferably not members of her own family.

When Leslie came in late one Friday night, her parents grounded her. It was like putting a lioness in a small cage and Leslie couldn't take it. After one day of confinement to the house, she ran away. The police picked her up two days later but she refused to go home unless someone would come along and "listen to her side of the story." Several family counseling sessions later Leslie got what she had wanted from the beginning—more liberal hours. Leslie's story illustrates one way that grounding can cause more trouble than it's worth. Her parents had started out well: they knew Leslie valued her free time and that the loss of her free time would be a serious blow. They grounded her because she was late, which was an appropriate linking of punishment to crime. But they had not spelled out this consequence in advance, and they did not set a definite limit to the restriction. Most teenagers don't run away, as Leslie did, but many kids will grump around the house making you wish they were somewhere else; so if you extend the restriction because of this rotten attitude, you also extend your own misery.

Grounding can be an effective form of discipline, but to make it work for you rather than against you, and most important to use it for the responsible growth of your children, I would suggest five basic "ground" rules.

First, let your kids know in advance what kind of behavior will result in grounding. Make it a logical consequence of certain very specific rule infractions: "The abuse of free time means the loss of free time. If you come home later than the hour we agree to before you go, that is an abuse of your free time. If you go someplace other than where you say you are going, that is an abuse of free time. And if you are not where you say you will be, that is an abuse of free time." (You will simplify things even more if you make it clear that lateness will be judged by the clock on your living room wall, not by your teenager's watch or his friend's car clock or the position of the moon in the sky.)

Second, always use the loss of free time as a consequence for the abuse of free time, and never as a consequence for something else. If your daughter fails to do her normal house chores, don't ground her—think of something more appropriate. (You can simply stand next to her pointing out the spots she has missed until she has cleaned the kitchen floor to your satsifaction.) But if the offense is related to free time, don't be talked into handing out a consequence other than the loss of free time. "If you're late, you lose your free time for a week. No, you can't do extra chores instead."

Third, set a definite ending date to the grounding period. Stay away from the "we'll see how you do" approach. You'll win more respect and change more behavior by being specific, certain, and firm.

Fourth, drop any future mention of the original offense. Who among us doesn't hate nippy little reminders of an old mistake? It's like being bitten to death by ducks.

And finally, you may have inadvertently or deliberately included the date of a major rock concert or an important high school festivity in the grounding period. Though it is tempting to hold your ground on that red-letter date, I'm convinced you can win more by letting your children win too: go ahead and give him a pass for that one evening. It's a simple act of grace, and it will surely be remembered.


## GUILTING

An even more common discipline technique, one used both by accident and by design, is guilting. My mother's tears guilted me on the way home from the store that day, though I don't believe she specifically intended them to. For some of us, a mother's tears—if they are rarely seen—can be powerful persuaders. A colleague of mine spent two years in a confirmation class which he had steadfastly refused to attend, simply because he couldn't stand to see his mother cry.

"I absolutely refused to go to confirmation. I drew the line at that. I wasn't gonna go. So she argued and we went back and forth, but I wouldn't budge. She threatened to take away my bicycle, warned me about what my father would do when he got home, and then she cried. And the minute she cried, I felt like a clod.

"So I went to confirmation, kicking rocks all the way. I was even confirmed. I had never made my mom cry before, and that really had an effect. I never told her how much I hated confirmation, but I told everybody else, and I proved my disgust by not learning anything and by cheating to get through. I bought off the girl next to me."

His story brought back old memories because I have taught confirmation. I can testify to the futility of goading, dragooning, or guilting kids into going to class against their will. A roomful of reluctant confirmands is indifference refined to the level of art. More young people are confirmed *out* of the church than into it in this manner.

All the same, guilting is commonly used either to get a teenager to do something he doesn't want to do or to make him regret something which he did because he wanted to. Parents often begin the process with a line like "How could you do this to us?" Then there is the wordless, withering look (some parents get by with the look alone) and the old cliché "We have always expected more from you."

This year a fifteen-year-old girl killed herself because she got a B on her report card. She had always gotten straight A's in school, and her parents were very upset when she fell below her usual performance. The story was reported nationally by the Associated Press.

Guilting can lead to disaster. It can also set kids up for time spent on an analyst's couch once they are adults trying to learn not to feel guilty about some perfectly normal desires. A teenager with a healthy conscience will feel naturally contrite if he has committed an act which upsets you; he will tie himself to the whipping post and he will brandish the whip. Your guilting will only be salt in his wounds. And if he doesn't have a healthy conscience, your guilting will have no effect on him one way or the other.

## CONTROL

Every parent's goal should be to get beyond punishment. Punishment becomes obsolete when you learn the principles of control. Many kids already know these principles and use them to manipulate every member of the family. The three-year-old boy at the meat counter knew how to control his mother. He got her to lose her temper, embarrass herself, and take time to escort him out to the car. And he did it all with a minimum of annoying behavior.

So I am not talking about control in the sense that one controls a robot, but about a powerful force which is much more subtle than that. I can explain it best by talking about the relationship between me and my dog.

Tawny is a rotund, blond cocker spaniel who has been called Fat Boy for most of his adult life. If I keep him on a leash when we go for a walk, he controls me by deciding when we stop and go, what direction we will take, and when some invisible scent on the grass is worth five minutes of our time. If I try to use force to tug him along, he sits down, sets his jaw, and roots himself to the ground. At that moment he is controlling our relationship. If I spank him and drag him along, I usually upset some bystander who doubtless thinks I am brutal and that Fat Boy is cute. This makes me even madder.

I enjoy our walks far more when I cross the street to a large fenced-in school yard. I unleash him and he romps off to investigate the shrubs at his own leisure. I have more fun and so does he. I don't get angry and he doesn't feel frustrated, and if I give him a reasonable amount of time on the loose, he will come when I call. Ironically, then, it is when I give him a measure of freedom that I also gain a measure of control. Fat Boy minds me better when he is off the leash than on it.

Parents and teenagers are also involved in a struggle to define their relationship with each other, to determine who is really in control. My duel with Fat Boy is one example; an incident from my adolescence will illustrate the principle further.

I had teased my sister unmercifully. Justice was both swift and uncompromising. I was without television privileges for one week.

Three days into that week I sneaked into the den, switched on the set, put the volume on low and sat down. Fifteen minutes later my father strolled in, looked at me and at the luminous picture tube, and with a no-quarter tone in his voice reminded me that four days remained on my sentence. I skulked out of the room. My father thus maintained control of our relationship. On the other hand, suppose he had walked into the den and thought, "That kid is testing me, but I'm too tired to argue with him today so I'll just let it go this time." His silence would have given me control of the situation. As he left the room without a word, my natural reaction would be to think, "Aha! I've won." And I would test him again the next chance I got. In precisely this way, many children gain almost complete control of their parents.

You needn't be hardnosed just to stay in control. Suppose my father had caught me watching television but felt that I had been particularly well behaved ever since the day I tortured my sister. He could then say, "You know you shouldn't be watching television, but you've had such a good attitude for the past three days that I'm willing to forget the rest of your punishment." He is still defining our relationship because he is *letting* me watch—it is his decision to make, not mine. He has refused to be manipulated by my defiance. But what is absolutely essential is that he take the time to say what he feels out loud; if he kept his thoughts to himself, I could have assumed that I had just won a contest of wills.

All this talk of control may sound a bit Machiavellian; actually it is a simple, thoughtful way of caring about your children—about what they do and about what kind of people they will become. No relationship is ever completely one-sided, although sometimes a parent will allow a relationship to become so neutral that it is meaningless. I met Mrs. Lee on the street several months ago and learned that she was worried because her daughter Ellen spent most of the day alone in the house with her boyfriend. It was summer, Mrs. Lee worked all day, and her husband was away on a military tour of duty. She felt that she had lost control of her daughter's actions.

I asked her to pinpoint her main concern: why did it bother her that Ellen was in the house all day without supervision? She told me it was "just the principle of the thing—the two of them in the house alone all the time." I asked her to be more specific about this "principle." What was it? She decided that she trusted Ellen to be alone in the house with the boy but she hated to see Ellen squander her whole summer. Why didn't she get out of the house, volunteer to work for some service organization or involve herself again with the church youth group. They were always doing interesting things.

With those feelings clarified, she confronted Ellen, explained her discomfort, and asked her to limit her time alone with the boyfriend to a couple of hours on any given day. She also showed Ellen a list of organizations that might need her help on a volunteer basis. Mrs. Lee was surprised when Ellen welcomed her suggestions and accepted the two-hour limit. She was getting bored with her do-nothing routine, and a week later she volunteered to work at a nearby drop-in center. Ellen had begun to think that her mother really didn't care what she did, and although she enjoyed the freedom she was also bothered by her mother's apparent indifference.

So what if Ellen had not reacted so cooperatively? There are two basic kinds of relationship you can have with another person. A complementary relationship is one in which one person gives advice and the other takes it, one person offers criticism and the other accepts it, one person gives an order and the other follows it. A symmetrical relationship is one in which two people both feel free to exchange ideas, to criticize each other, to suggest and initiate action.

When Ellen accepted her mother's time limit, their relationship was complementary. If she had refused the time limit, she would be saying, in effect, "I don't want you to come to me with rules that I've had no say in." She would be insisting that where rules are concerned, she wants a symmetrical relationship. Mrs. Lee could then say, "All right, let's see if we can compromise. I am uncomfortable with the amount of time you spend here in the house each day, with or without John. I feel there must be better things to do with your summer." Unless Ellen is completely incorrigible, she will work with her mother toward a solution to the problem, and this process of working together, explaining feelings, giving here and standing firm there, is often far more important than the final result.

The real Ellen did accept her mother's time limit but she didn't like any of her mother's ideas for volunteer work. They brainstormed for a while and Ellen came up with the idea of the drop-in center. Mrs. Lee had heard the center was infested with "hippies," but she didn't press the issue. At that point, the mother-daughter relationship was symmetrical. No relationship is always complementary or always symmetrical; we go back and forth between them depending on our needs.

## CONTRACTING

Another concept which goes beyond discipline is contracting. Many parents make informal contracts with their teenagers: if you mow the lawn, you can go out Saturday night. A boy named Jeff and his parents had a running dispute about the length of his hair. The father particularly loathed his son's hair, and even though Jeff kept it clean and combed, it was a gut issue not subject to normal reasoning. Still, Jeff's parents were not the type to force him to get it cut—it had to happen some other way.

During ninth grade, Jeff turned into a ski fanatic. He took part-time jobs, squirreled his money away, and used every penny for equipment and tow tickets when the snows came. As that first ski winter passed into summer, Jeff's hair reached his collar bone, and he continued to save carefully for the next ski season. By November he was watching the weather reports like a farmer with newly-sown fields. At that precise moment his parents made him an offer he couldn't refuse: Thanksgiving weekend in Aspen with two good friends who lived there—if he would cut his hair to a more reasonable length. They didn't expect a Marine butch, they just wanted to see the bottoms of his ears. The offer was so attractive that Jeff felt no remorse when he took his seat in the barber's chair.

In essence, Jeff's parents made a contract with him: if you cut your hair, we will send you to Aspen for Thanksgiving. Something was given and something was gotten, and the contract worked because Jeff's parents were sensitive to his dreams; they knew three days in Aspen would be a powerful reward.

Many family therapists use a more formal version of contracting to help repair parent-child relationships. And since it is not a secret formula, you can make good use of the contract idea on your own. You needn't wait until you are facing a tense situation, although the contract works well in a crisis.

To begin, you will need two lists. One should be written by your son or daughter, and it should include all those things he or she likes to do most. The other is a list of the things you expect of your teenager during an ordinary week and during an ordinary day. Be specific. If you want him to mow the lawn every Saturday morning, write it down. If you want him home by midnight every Saturday night, put that down too. If he has certain chores to complete after dinner each night, list them. And if you want him to hang up his clothes rather than strew them around the house, spell that out.

Then sit down together with your lists and two blank sheets of paper. Suppose his list of likes includes playing pinball, watching television, spending time with his friends, listening to rock music, and eating chocolate chip ice cream. Your aim will be to link each of your expectations to a specific reward. "If you mow the lawn every Saturday morning, you can spend the afternoon and the evening with your friends. How does that sound to you?" If you agree, you both write the agreement down as the first item in your contract. If you meet resistance, try linking the expected behavior with a more powerful reward, but don't get sidetracked—you must make it clear that each of the desired activities will have to be earned. Most contracts go rather easily. "If you are home by midnight every Saturday night, you can stay out until midnight the next Saturday night and we'll throw in some pinball money." Get an agreement and write it down. "If you hang your clothes up and we never see them lying around the house, then you can listen to your music for an hour every day and once a month we'll give you the money to buy a new album. If you do your after-dinner chores without being reminded each day, you can watch television and we'll keep a half-gallon of chocolate chip ice cream on hand."

Once you have agreed on each point and you have both written down what you've said, sign each copy at the bottom. It's best, of course, if both parents are involved in the process so that three signatures go on the bottom of the contracts. You include a definite time limit for the contract: "We'll try this for two months [or six months, or two weeks—whatever works]. Then we'll sit down again and review each point. If something needs to be changed, we'll talk it over then."

If you draw up contracts with your kids, one of the first benefits you will notice is how much work it does for you. Let's say your daughter comes home late Saturday night without a reasonable excuse. You are saved the trouble of working out a response. An agreement has been signed, and it is clear that coming home late means house restriction the next weekend. It's all down in black and white.

Naturally contracts fall apart. It may be only one part of the contract that fails, or it may be the whole agreement. If this happens you sit down and renegotiate. What went wrong? Maybe a birthday has come and gone and your teenager feels his curfew should be relaxed. Or maybe one of the rewards in the contract no longer has meaning for him. Don't give up on the concept if it fails the first time, just start from scratch and draw up another contract.

Clever kids will try to lead you away from the immediate job, which is linking expectations to specific rewards. You can plan on a line like "Why do *I* have to do this? Sally gets to do whatever she wants." Don't be diverted. "Right now we're talking about *you*. I'll be talking with Sally later on." Another favorite line in families where the kids have had lots of free rein is "I never had to do anything to get these things before. Why are you changing it around now?" Stick to the details of making the contract and try not to get into an argument. Let's face it, in the real world few people get something for nothing. It's good for young people to sign a contract and live up to it. And even under the contract system, kids do have a choice—they don't *have* to do what they've agreed to do. But if they don't, they'll miss the rewards, rewards which you have made sure are important to them, and life is likely to be rather dull.

The contract includes many of the qualities most needed in parent-teenager relations: it is specific, it is above-board, it is based on positive reinforcement, and it is down in writing. If it sounds too cold and businesslike to you, don't use it. You can use the principles of contracting even when you don't commit your agreements to a piece of paper. And if you do try formal contracting, remember there is always lots of room for the plain, human give-and-take that is the essence of the heart-to-heart talk.

## THE HEART-TO-HEART TALK

Teenagers I have known vote unanimously for a heart-to-heart talk with father or mother (but not with both) as the most behavior-changing experience of their adolescence. One girl says of her father, "By talking to me, he made me feel more like an adult, not like a kid being taken aside to be spanked. He made me feel that he understood, and that I could level with him. That was a big change and because of it, I don't think I ever lied to my dad."

When a relationship between parent and child is based mainly on the use of pressure points, it isn't much of a relationship. What every parent wants is love and respect, and the same is true of every teenager. Mutual respect means that you work hard to set rules and make requests which take into account the maturity, the dignity, and the individuality of your children; it also means that they work hard to obey the rules you have made, even the ones they don't like. And, in fact, this is exactly what happens in most families for most of the time.

When a teenager breaks a rule his parents have laid down, he often does it because he believes the rule is beneath him, that it demeans him, that it shows how little his parents respect him, his judgment, his morality, and his need for a larger share of independence. Once again the issues of trust and respect are the crux of all those arguments over whether Sally should be allowed to stay out an hour later on Friday and Saturday nights.

So when a rule is broken, your best move is to talk it over with your teenager. Is the rule reasonable? Is it a fair rule for a thirteen-year-old but not for a fifteen-year-old? If it is a bad rule, how might it be changed? When you ask questions like these out loud during a discussion with your teenager, you will change the nature of your relationship with him. You are no longer the omnipotent parent issuing orders that are to be instantly obeyed. You are one person talking with another person. Even though that other person is still your child and you are still the authority figure, you are trying to break through those roles so that you can better understand each other.

You and your spouse will need to decide which parent is to have this talk with your teenager. The most comfortable choice, decided on the basis of which of you already has the closest rapport, will probably mean a mother-son or a father-daughter talk. But the parent who stays behind will miss out on what may be a life-shaping experience. A more significant breakthrough occurs when the parent with the *least* rapport asks for a long talk on a feeling level. So decide which of you is to ask for the talk on the basis of what your own needs are, together with the subjects that need discussing, and the current status of the relationships each of you has with your child.

Even a serious family crisis like a son arrested for drugs or a daughter expelled from school can be converted into a bond of understanding by means of a long talk. You may find yourself dispensing with your old caricatures and struggling with a new intimacy you haven't experienced before. You may not be able to put all your feelings into words—few people ever can or even want to. Just remember that after a gut-level talk with a parent many kids come away feeling that some rare kind of understanding has been reached and that from now on, life will be better.

How do you start this kind of talk? Try giving voice to the strongest feeling you have. One father, more hurt than angry with his daughter, began a long talk with "I'd like to say I understand why you did it, but I really don't. It's got me confused because it doesn't seem like you. Maybe I haven't been paying enough attention to who you are and what you're really like these days, but I want to pay attention now." He didn't know what would happen next. What did happen was a long and beautiful dialogue.

Kids want more freedom and need both direction and structure. I hope this chapter will help you as a parent give your own children all three. I have said nothing of physical punishment because I believe it belittles both the punisher and the punished. More important, I believe it is so very important to reach beyond punishment of any kind. The beauty of the contract is that punishment is redefined as the loss of privileges, not the piling on of extra and onerous chores.

It's also important to know that there is a lot of room for mistakes, and that few mistakes do any real damage. Consider these memoirs of a young man who today is a mature responsible person:

"I was never caught smoking, drinking, smoking dope, or taking pills. I never did anything wrong that my parents knew of. If I was going to smoke a joint, I made sure I had some Visine with me so that when I walked in the door, my eyes wouldn't be bloodshot—little tricks like that. Wash your hands before you go home so you won't smell like smoke, put the cigarettes down the crotch when you walk by them. Have a good alibi laid out. I was lucky, I never got caught by the police for shoplifting or anything else, even though I was doing all that stuff."

Kind of puts this whole business in perspective, doesn't it? He got away with a lot, maybe too much for his own good, but the observable fact is that he turned out all right and has a great future. I think there is a big lesson in that fact. Discipline is an easy subject to take too seriously. Montaigne wrote in his *Essays,* "There is no course of life so weak and sottish as that which is managed by order, method, and discipline." His words rattle my cage because no author can finish a book without using order, method, and discipline. For that matter, a kid who washes his hands after smoking, puts Visine in his eyes, and has a good alibi laid out is using order, method, and discipline. But the truth in what Montaigne says is clear: most of us learn best when we are given the space to make our own mistakes and to win our own victories. If we don't get that space, we are likely to grow up feeling small and captured—and to be that kind of adult.

A syndicated advice-giver once said that being a parent doesn't mean you are a rug to be stepped on. True enough. But neither does it mean you are a portrait in oils, required always to wear the same stolid expression!

# 6

# Running Away

This year at least half a million teenagers will run away from home. In just one respect, that's good: more than a million kids were on the run each year during the late sixties and the early seventies, so the numbers have leveled off and dropped. Many of the young people who ran away during the flower days were not really running away from their homes, they were running to some alluring place. For at least half of those kids, the primary motive was adventure and they ran to the East Village or to Haight-Ashbury, Taos, New Mexico, or Boulder, Colorado, hoping to find it.

By 1974 the kids who were running more for a lark than for a reason had dropped off, and today the runaways are more lost, more hurt, and more troubled than ever. They represent every race and class in society. They are still running from both the worst and the best of homes, but they are running because they feel they really need to run. And they are younger. The average age for runaway children in 1970 was fifteen; today it is between thirteen and fourteen, according to the latest FBI statistics. That means the most typical runaway in America today is a fourteen-year-old girl. Yes, more girls than boys run away from home these days, and it is a growing trend.

That "typical" girl will be on the run for two days to two months. If she is lucky and smart, she will wind up seeking help from a runaway house: The Looking Glass in Chicago, The Truck Stop in Atlanta, Huckleberry House in San Francisco, The Bridge in Minneapolis, or Runaway House in Washington, D.C., to name only a few. The young people who show up at these places get professional help and a safe bed. Most of them go back to their parents with the name of a good home-town family counselor.

But runaway houses see only a small minority of the teenagers who run. Most kids hide out with friends or casual acquaintances, some of them hitchhike for hundreds of miles, and a small fraction of the total will rub shoulders with one or more of the world's certified, on-the-loose crazies. The most aimless kids are the most susceptible to danger and exploitation, but out of close to three hundred runaways I have counseled, only two had violent experiences. Despite the serious problems many of them faced at home, the vast majority had a good time while they were on the run.

Most parents want the answers to three questions. Why do kids run? What can a parent do to lower the chance that one of his own children will join the crowd? And what do you do if he runs anyway? The first question is the most important one because once you know why, you often know what to do next. Whatever you do, don't think it could never happen in your family; "We've never had any trouble before" is the first thing many parents say when they start calling around, hoping to get a lead on their runaway teenagers.

## WHY DO THEY RUN?

On the surface you'll find a hundred different reasons. A boy knows he is failing most of his classes and doesn't want to stick around to face the evidence. A girl thinks she is pregnant and is afraid to tell her mother. A kid selling dope thinks he is about to be busted. Some kids still take off without any heavy reasons; adventure, a change of pace, and the promise of fun and freedom are reason enough. But most runaways leave home because they resent the rules their parents have set.

And running away is easier today than it was ten or twenty years ago. Most teenagers know before they leave home that they can get a night's safe lodging and an open ear through any drop-in center or crisis line. These services exist in order to reduce the number of runaway kids who fall prey to pimps and muggers, and they are there to serve as a reconciling force if they can. The services were created in response to a rising tide of runaways back in the sixties, and the

Runaway Youth Act of 1974 will pump ten million dollars a year, through 1977, into an expansion of the current services available to runaway children and their families. If one of your kids runs away, you'll be glad the shelter care facilities and the counselors are there to help—but it's also true that their very existence may add strength to the growing resolve of an unhappy teenager who is thinking of running. He knows he won't be alone out there, and that makes his decision a little easier.

In a typical group of ten runaways, two or three will be extreme cases. There are at least two types of extremes: one is a selfish, spoiled brat who left home expecting the world to give him tea and sympathy; the other is a bruised and desperate kid, on the run from indifferent parents who never liked their children much, not even on the day they were born.

The spoiled kids are often, though not always, suburban products. They use embarrassment to blackmail their parents. The most important difference between cities and suburbs is that the walls are thinner in the cities; your neighbors know what's happening whether you want them to or not. But suburban people, living in single-family homes, can be great pretenders. "Oh, everything is just fine with us!" Suburban kids know they are likely to embarrass their parents if they run, and if they are clever manipulators they will try to cash in on that embarrassment.

The battered kids come from every economic level, and they need all the help the courts can give them. Taking a child away from his parents is a serious business in this country, and it should be. The law requires blatant evidence of brutality before the court will take custody of a runaway teenager, so these kids are often sent home. They run away again and again until, finally, someone takes them seriously.

If all runaways were either spoiled or battered, we would still have a problem but we wouldn't have an epidemic. Yet we still have tens of thousands of kids on the run from good homes, from parents who love their children and want to help. The kids themselves are good kids, but something has gone wrong in the family and no one had the right words at the right time, so they ran. I believe there are four underlying reasons why we still have so many runaway children, reasons which apply to almost all of us.

The first reason is the modern trend toward *smaller families*. The natural jolts and bumps between family members were more easily absorbed when families were larger and stayed in one place. Grandparents were usually the best shock absorbers, followed by uncles, aunts, and older children still living at home. When Suzie got mad at her mother, she could air her gripes with a grandparent; when father gave more attention to his business than to his sons and daughters, a grandfather, uncle, or older brother filled the vacuum. Kids could always con a kindly aunt into pleading their case on those sticky issues they could never win by themselves.

If you say I'm idealizing the past, you're absolutely right. But families did have more built-in pressure valves then, and when they worked, children felt no need to leave home before it was time to leave. We also looked more kindly, many years ago, on the sixteen-year-old who packed up, left home, and tried to begin a life of his own. A kid like that was not a runaway, he was resourceful.

Our families have grown smaller, mobility has increased, and the natural tensions within families have become more intense. Hundreds of miles often separate us from our parents, brothers, and sisters. Two children, conceived under the otherwise sensible notion that two is enough for any family on an overcrowded planet, now must carry the expectations we once divided between four, six, and occasionally ten or twelve children in families of yesteryear. Too many expectations lead to frustration, anger, and a feeling of helplessness: "I just can't be what they want me to be!" cries the teenager, who should surprise no one when he finally turns and runs.

This introduces a second underlying reason for runaways: many kids feel *powerless* in their own homes in front of their own parents. Most runaways are impressively self-perceptive. Sage, a fifteen-year-old girl who showed up at one center late one afternoon worn out after three days on the run, wanting a place to stay for the night, had this to say about her parents: "They spoiled the hell out of me when I was little and now they're trying to make up for it all at once. I feel like a prisoner when I'm at home."

She turned out to be a good judge both of herself and of her parents. Sage is the youngest child in her family and her parents have a bad case of "our baby" disease. She is a sensible and responsible person for her age, but at home she was never given a chance to prove it. Lots of kids run away from less than that. Much less. Like arguments over hair, clothes, rock music, and other minor issues that always look ridiculous in retrospect; some young girls leave home because their parents refuse to let them wear jeans!

When children have no power, when they never win an argument with you, never get a concession from you, when they feel that the cards at home are permanently marked against them, then running away becomes their only hope of changing the rules. And remember that we are no longer talking about the super-spoiled extremes, but about the other seven or eight runaways in that typical group of ten. They leave home because they feel powerless, because they are not allowed to prove that they are capable of being responsible; and when they run, their parents point to their act as living proof of their irresponsibility. "Just like I've been telling you, the first big thing she can't have her own way on and poof! she takes off." If you have ever been in that parent's shoes, you may have said something like that, and you may have been absolutely right. The trouble is that it doesn't solve anything. Blaming never does.

Overprotective *love* is a third common situation producing runaways. The kids leave home because they are fighting for air, because their parents over-protect them either by asking too many questions or by patronizing them with a shallow and uncritical love. It is a thin line for any parent to walk: to ask enough questions and to ask them in such a way that you show the interest you genuine.y feel, and at the same time to keep from asking too many questions that will seem, to your teenager, to be nosey and inappropriate. It is equally true that uncritical love is just another form of indifference, and that a long series of leading questions work best not in your home but where they belong—on the Perry Mason re-runs.

You will be wise to be careful with your last-born son or daughter. Some kids like being last, and the last child is often the most spoiled, a fact he will admit if pressed. Once all of his brothers and sisters have moved out and gone on to jobs, marriages, or college, he may enjoy having the family spotlight to himself. He may also be the type who can't stand the glare.

*Discrimination against daughters* is the fourth major cause of runaways. We tend to restrict and protect our daughters much more than our sons. We ask more questions after a date, we give them tighter hours, and we allow them fewer opportunities, compared to our sons, to demonstrate the responsibility of which they are often capable. In fact, we have known for years that girls mature more quickly than boys and need to be given responsibility and trust at an earlier age, but in practice we do just the opposite. It is no accident that the most typical runaway is a fifteen-year-old girl.

A survey conducted by my former counseling agency shows that most high school boys feel no serious tensions with their parents except in their eleventh grade year—the year they get their driver's licenses. But the girls indicate a steady, undiminishing tension betweeen themselves and their parents from tenth through twelfth grade. Most girls don't go so far as to run away, but they do feel their brothers are treated more liberally. Usually, they're right.

## WHAT YOU CAN DO

We can't stop the trend toward smaller families, but we can do something about children who feel powerless, about smother love, and about daughters who feel discriminated against. Even if you think your family has one of these symptoms, you can benefit by running a power check on each member in it. Who has most of the power? When Suzie wants special permission for something, who does she go to? If mother says, "Ask your father," and father says, "Ask your mother," it may be that the kids themselves have most of the family power. In some families the "good" kids have a corner on most of the power; in subtle ways they encourage their "bad" brother or sister to keep on getting into trouble, thus diverting parental attention from their own misdeeds. If you can't pinpoint the power in your family, ask your youngest child who he thinks has most of it; like the catcher on a baseball team, he has the clearest view of everyone in the family.

Once you've done a power check, you may see a need to distribute power more evenly among family members. The loudest objections to this idea will come from whoever already has most of it; democracy is not an easy concept for countries or families that have always been ruled by dictators. It's also startling to discover, as many families do, that the real dictator is not mother or father but a four-year-old child who has learned how to make everyone else in the family bow to his every wish. No matter where the power lies, when a family begins to decide together by a majority vote its rules, discipline techniques, vacation plans, and curfew hours, power will be as evenly distributed as is humanly possible. Best of all, you are much less likely to ever have to worry about runaway children.

You may be reading this chapter because you have a teenager on the run right now. If so, you are wondering if you have tried every possible source of information: your son or daughter's closest friends, any local agencies set up specifically to shelter runaways, other youth help organizations like drop-in centers, hotlines, and counseling services. Many parents also wonder if they should call the police.

When twenty-four hours have passed without a word, a call to the police can't do any harm. First offense runaways are routinely returned to their parents in most communities, so police contact won't mean the beginning of a court record. It will mean that you have a few more eyes on the lookout. On the other hand, if you know your teenager is staying somewhere nearby, asking the police to pick him up is likely to stir resentment and deter reconciliation. If you've heard that Johnny is staying in the treehouse behind the old Parsons place, simply pass the word through his friends that he is welcome home whenever he's ready, and let him make the next move. The youth agency closest to your home can be your best ally. The youth workers in your own neighborhood will know the territory better than anyone and they may know kids who will have inside information. Remember that your teenager's friends are honor-bound by an unwritten code to tell you, the parent, nothing, but they might share what they know with a youth counselor.

Waiting is the hardest part for parents because in the end there is very little you can do. You want to hear something, but you can't order the phone to ring with good news, and you can't totally erase those mental images of terrible forces beyond your control coming down on top of your wayward child. Once you've talked with the youth agencies and with your son or daughter's friends, you'll do yourself a favor if you try to relax. In a sense, kids who run away want their parents to find out what it's like to be powerless, to be stuck in a painful situation with no way out until someone else makes a move.

Of course a runaway wants you to want him back. If you just yawned and went about your business as usual, half the point of running would be lost. One girl told me, "They're not even *trying* to find me! Now I know for sure they don't give a damn about me!"

If you're obsessed by visions of disaster while waiting to hear something, you might remember that most runaways have a great time. Even those kids who spend a couple of cold, damp nights sleeping in the woods usually look back on their run as a grand adventure. They remember it as their first delicious taste of absolute freedom. Runaways love to gab about their on-the-road experiences. After all, running away is as American as Mark Twain, and unlike Huck Finn, today's kids have plenty of people who will help them get from island to island.

## SPECIAL COUNSELING

If you do have a runaway teenager, you may want to get some help from a family counselor once he is home again. There are all kinds, and if you ask around you'll find that some of the best ones are either free (because they work for a government agency) or will adjust their fees to meet your budget. Sometimes your feelings and the feelings of your teenager are like a log jam at a river bend, and a counselor can usually help you get unstuck and on your way again.

Sue and her parents are a good example. She ran away because "I want to make more of my own decisions, like when I should come home, when I should study, and who I can be with." She stayed with a girl friend and even went to school during the five days she was "on the run." Her parents knew she was in school but didn't know where she was staying. They judiciously resisted their temptation to have her picked up while she was sitting in one of her classes.

On the fifth day of her self-imposed exile from home, Sue called me to arrange a meeting with her parents "on neutral ground." I set up the meeting and had a chance to talk to her alone for a few minutes before her parents arrived. She was fifteen then, dedicated to getting a good education, very level-headed in all that she had to say. I wondered about the risk she had taken by going to school— most kids on the run would have stayed in hiding.

"Did you want your parents to catch you and bring you home?" I asked. Well, she really did want to go home, but before she did she wanted her old man to bend a little, just once. I also knew that Sue enjoyed drinking and that her parents were teetotalers. They had caught her with alcohol on her breath a couple of times and had restricted her to the house for weeks after each occasion.

Sue's father has a resonant, rolling voice worthy of a Baptist preacher, and when he arrived for our meeting he felt that he had to use it to deliver a long, dusty sermon. Sue tuned him out after his first sentence—the tone in his voice told her all she needed to know. When I stopped him and pointed out that Sue had stopped listening, he seemed neither hurt nor surprised. Sue's mother had to step in and suggest the compromise which made it possible for her to go home with them that night.

Fortunately Sue got an honest chance to set her own schedule and the experiment was a beautiful success until one Saturday night. She came home drunk and got caught. We had another session together and it was clear that Sue wanted to get caught that night. She loved her parents, particularly her father, but he paid her little heed even when they were involved in a direct conversation. Drinking and running away were Sue's way of getting his attention. He loves her, but he is a tight, conservative man, born in Scandinavia and made of stubborn stuff. He has always given his children everything he knows how to: a roof, food on the table, and absolute loyalty to their mother.

At the age of sixteen, Sue learned that however much she wanted a more obvious display of love from her father, he is what he is and will never change; once she understood that, she accepted it—she let what he could be, be enough—and she accepted herself.

## LETTING GO

Some kids run away because they want their independence, and often the best thing you can do is give it to them. Sherry disappeared from her home in the middle of a Minnesota February with nothing but a light coat to protect her from twenty below zero temperatures. A group of college friends took her in, and she called her mother the next day to say she was all right and that she didn't want to come home.

Five weeks passed, mother and daughter had several phone conversations, but nothing was resolved. Sherry's mother wanted her sixteen-year-old daughter back home and in school. Then Sherry called and asked me to set up a face-to-face conference with her mother. I had never met either of them.

I chose a small church for their meeting, and when they got together they hugged and cried and their tears nearly froze in the icy parking lot. Once inside, they tried to lay out the issues. Sherry loved her mother fully as much as she herself was loved, but she wanted more than her mother's love. She wanted her blessing, no cops, no more pleading, and the right to come home for visits without feeling like a renegade. Sherry was determined to make it on her own, to get a job and a place that was all hers.

"But you're only sixteen. Think of all the time you've got ahead to do what you want."

"Mom, that's like saying, 'You don't have the numbers yet.' The numbers aren't important. *I* am important!"

"Don't you realize how difficult it's going to be? What are you going to do without a high school degree?"

"I'll take correspondence courses, I'll get my degree. I want it as much as you want me to have it."

"I just wish you would come home with me."

"Mom, just because I want to leave home two years earlier than most kids do doesn't mean you've done anything wrong! I'm not like all the other kids."

"I just don't know if I can stand to let you go. I haven't slept in the last five weeks, worrying about you."

She began to cry, resting her head on the table, her body shaking with the effort to hold back her feelings. Sherry watched her mother, her own tears gathered at the corners of her eyes, but she controlled them. More than anything in the world at that moment she wanted to appear strong, to prove to her mother that she was ready, that she could handle her own freedom. Two years later, looking back on that day, her eyes misted as she told me, "It's really hard to be sixteen and to want to be on your own."

They argued for another hour, but in the end Sherry got her

mother's blessing—and, mysteriously, the bond between mother and daughter was deepened.

Spring came that year and Sherry was doing fine. I met her mother one day on the street and told her how strong she had been that winter day. I asked her what had finally brought her to the conclusion that she should let Sherry go, and have always prized her answer.

"I never felt that I owned Sherry or any of my kids. I wanted her home because I loved her, and I let her go because I respected her."

Half of a parent-child relationship is love and the other half is respect. Without both of them, we lose the chance ever to know each other.


## SHELTER CARE HOMES

I helped staff a home for runaway youth in Boulder, Colorado, during the summer of 1974. Our purpose began with the basics: food, a hot shower, and a clean bed. The kids were always starved when they got to us, and no wonder. Most of them had eaten little more than the occasional hamburger during several days of cross-country hitchhiking. They had obviously left home in a hurry because they rarely had more with them than the clothes they wore.

Once a kid had eaten and showered and taken some time to tell his story, we had him call home. That was an absolute rule of the house. The phone conversations were always emotional, and it was amazing how many parents and kids reconciled their differences long distance. A thousand miles from home most kids had gotten in touch with how much they really loved their parents. And while the kids were getting halfway across the country, their parents were getting in touch with how much they loved their kids. All that was needed in many, many cases was an affirmation of that love on both sides.

Sometimes the affirmation never came. Instead, the message was "We're better off without you." The police had tagged these kids with a sad and fitting name: throwaways. Whenever times are hard financially, runaway homes have a high percentage of kids who are actually throwaways.

Most runaways never leave their own home town, and shelter care facilities do their best work with the local kids, if given the chance. The law says that the staff at any runaway home must call the parents within a specified period of time—usually twenty-four hours after the kid arrives. Most teenagers who leave home during a conflict *need* time to cool down.

Albert is a kid from Illinois who had just made it to Colorado when the police picked him up and brought him in. The Colorado police are unusually adept in spotting runaways. Albert's father arranged air fare for the next day, and he was packed off to Moline before he had even seen a real mountain. I had a strong feeling that Albert would take off the next chance he got, and an equally strong feeling that if his dad had let him stay with us for a few days, Albert's craving for a change of scene would have been satisfied.

It's hard to bide your time and lèt the counselors do their job, especially when the runaway house that has your kid is just a short drive across town rather than several states away. But if you can communicate a double message—that you want your teenager back and that you're willing to take whatever time is needed to work through his feelings and your own—I can virtually guarantee that the return home will work better for all of you.

When a return seems impossible, either to you or your teenager or to both of you, it is time to consider

## FOSTER PARENTS

"But if we let some other family take him, we'll be admitting failure." That is the gut feeling. Pride. Angry parents would see their child go to a detention center rather than agree to a foster placement. If he goes to an institution, people will assume it is the kid's fault, but if he goes to a foster home people think his natural parents are lacking somehow.

I once wondered, in the world-wide community of parents who have teenagers, who would cast the first stone? Surely no one, I thought. But although stones went out a century ago, people of all faiths, colors, and creeds are still good at casting aspersions. So if you should find yourself in a situation where temporary foster placement seems the best solution to a problem you have with one of your teenagers, be prepared to make a tough, pride-swallowing decision.

Some runaways should not return to their homes for a few months; some need as much as a year or two away. Distance offers perspective, and when the picky day-by-day arguments are gone, the important issues have a chance to rise to the surface.

"But a foster home sounds so drastic." Actually, granting the exception of sending a teenager home with a recommendation for out-patient counseling, a foster home is the least drastic solution the courts can provide. And a foster placement need not suggest blame. Parents who have done well with their first two children may find they get nowhere with their third. The vibes are bad, as they say— nothing works, and the best intended remarks are interpreted as insults. When coexistence under one roof makes everyone in the house miserable, six months to a year in a foster home can be the most valuable, least expensive therapy a teenager and his parents will ever get.

Carol and her parents reached that point. Away from home she was considerate, soft-spoken, and self-perceptive; she knew her failings and admitted them with a smile. Around her parents she was a wench, and they played by Old Testament rules around her house: an eye for an eye. Most of the fighting centered on Carol's freaky boyfriend.

The court assigned Carol to a foster home during her senior year in high school because she had run away from home twice during the summer. She had regular visits with her natural parents and although politeness was the rule, the chemistry between them was clearly wrong. Meanwhile she had grown to love her foster parents and was a willing participant in the duties and benefits of her new life. She graduated with honors, found a good job, and eighteen months passed before she felt right about going home to stay for a while. Like many troubled young people, she needed time to think and grow, to see her parents in a new light, and to put some space between herself and the quarrels that had made life with her parents impossible.

Carol went home again; Jamie never did. She was a tough, plucky little fourteen-year-old when we met. She had been hiding in parks for five days. Her father died when she was ten and she joined the dopers at school when she went to junior high. Her "boyfriend" was a twenty-five-year-old man. But for all her worldly ways, Jamie was a favorite with her teachers, a solid B student working close to her capacity. The only course she hated was history, but she worked hard at it to prove that nothing could get her down.

I asked her why she had run away. She gave me no long list of gripes, no tales of abuse, no badmouthing. All she said, and she said it without a trace of emotion, was "I hate my mother, and I'm never going back there again, no matter what." When she talked just to pass the time, Jamie avoided eye contact, but when she said, "I'm never going back there again," she looked right at me. The court's final recommendation of a foster home was less a judgment against Jamie's mother than a recognition of the girl's cold resolve. If they had sent her home, she would have run again at the first opportunity.

Two years have passed and Jamie still refuses to do much talking about her past. The first fourteen years of her life sit in her past like an abandoned mine; maybe they should. In her foster home she loves and is loved, and for kids like Jamie that's all that really matters.

For a few young people, a foster home means a whole new life. For most kids it's a breathing space, a time to sort things out and do some thinking about the mother and father with whom they don't get along. Some will run from their foster homes as well. They discover that household chores and weekend hours are about the same no matter where you are, that life has certain inescapable responsibilities, and that it is unfair to blame parents just because they are the ones who remind us of those responsibilities. Most teenagers who spend a few months in a foster home grow in ways that would have been impossible in their own homes, and that is why you as a parent should be willing to consider foster placement as a possible solution, not an embarrassment.

## TRAINING SCHOOLS

We used to call them reform schools. There are some very bad ones. And even the very good ones have trouble winning the everyday fight against overcrowded dorms and unfortunate mixing of hardened delinquents with kids whose worst offense was to run away or cut school. But in many states the training schools do a good job of combining school work, group analysis, and individual therapy for troubled teenagers. The rule of thumb is to keep kids out of the juvenile justice system if you can, but some kids need to be sentenced for their own good and ours.

Donna needed a residential treatment center on the day she ran away. Aged fourteen, she could lie to her best friend without blinking, she dined on school counselors and ate social workers for dessert. If you put an empathetic counselor into the same room with her she was like a wily old fisherman, playing out her line and reeling it back in, working her hook in deeper each time.

Three runs in four months had given Donna a lot of power at home. She had her parents on that fishing line too, and she wasn't about to let them go. When the probation officer suggested that she ought to go to the state training school, she cried for her parents and they begged the judge to let them take her home. The reason Donna wanted to go home? There, she could get away with a life of total self-indulgence. If her parents displeased her she walked out on them; if a class at school bored her she skipped it; if an appointment with her probation officer threatened to interrupt a sunny afternoon or beer drinking with friends, she broke the appointment without a word.

Finally a judge gave Donna six weeks in a training school. He could have saved his breath and the taxpayers' money; Donna needed at least a year's mandatory stay. She needed to know that she couldn't con her way out, that she would have to live with it and listen to what the counselors and the other kids were telling her.

When she got to the school she was given the usual treatment for newcomers, a rough and ready dose of reality. The other teenagers watched her for a while, spotted the games she used to get her way, and then shoved them down her throat.

"You think you're too good to be here," a girl told her.

"You been jivin' people so long you don't know what the truth is," said a boy one year younger than Donna.

"You ain't levelin' with us, and that's why you ain't ever gonna level with yourself," said another.

No one had ever held up a mirror for Donna and said, "Take a good, long look at yourself, baby." And for most teenagers the reality treatment—dished out by other kids, not by the staff—is a serious jerk-around. Tough kids have gone into the program determined not to let it touch them and have come out six months to a year later with genuine skills in self-analysis and in working with other young people. But Donna buried her head like an ostrich and six weeks later, when the judge's order ran out and she went home, her lips were still in full pout.

The crisis created by a runaway child can be treated as a unique opportunity to learn. A certain amount of family tension is normal, and the kids who run from that tension are often the most sensitive members of the family. If given the chance, a runaway can tell you a lot about how the family operates. He knows about the brother who seems to care only about himself, the sister who doesn't pull her own weight with the chores, the father who never admits he is wrong, and the mother who lets everyone walk over her and then complains about it.

Changing a crisis into an opportunity to grow means you have to be willing to risk a change in the family order, perhaps a different method for making rules and assigning in-house responsibilities. But whatever happens, when you start talking with all of your children about how the family works, about who has the power, who shoulders the weight, who picks up the pieces, who apologizes first, who does the caretaking, the insights you gain are a therapeutic goldmine.

I look back and realize this is a chapter full of girls. Perhaps eighty percent of the runaways I have known personally are girls, and compared to the boys they seemed to have run for deeper reasons. Boys take off "because my old man hassles me all the time, especially about my hair." They rarely talk about the underlying vacuum, the need for a closer and warmer relationship with their fathers, the struggle to be liked or at least accepted "for myself, not for some image he has in his head of what I *should* be like." When the boys do start talking, the feelings are all there, but we have taught males in our culture to keep their feelings to themselves and, for the most part, that is what they do. That may be part of the reason why runaway boys tend to go farther and stay away longer than the girls do.

One final thought. Kids do love to talk about their adventures while they were on the run, but the people who ususally hear all these stories are friends, youth workers, and perhaps a favorite teacher at school. If one of your children ever runs away, wait until the dust has settled to get your own private telling. He'll try to put you off, of course.

"Wasn't much. Just a lot of standin' around waitin' for rides and then lookin' for a place to sleep."

But if you persist, he may overcome his natural reluctance to share an evil deed with the very people against whom it was perpetrated. If he does, he will probably give you a rendition far less flamboyant than the one he gave his friends. Even his edited version will be an odyssey well worth the telling and the listening.

# 7

---

# Sex

Most parents like to talk with their teenagers about love, and hate to talk to them about sex. An astonishing number of young people have never had a single discussion with either of their parents about sex, even on an elementary biological level. Yet most teenagers do want to talk with their parents, they do have serious questions to ask, and they sometimes get into even more serious trouble because they never had a chance to get the answers.

A few parents steel themselves for "that talk," but they are rarely confident about what to say or even how to bring the subject up. One medical doctor with four children gave the responsibility to his wife. As each of the kids reached puberty she asked, "Do you have any questions?" Each one said, "No," and that was the end of it.

A seventeen-year-old girl remembers her parents' attempt this way: "They talked with me separately when I was about eleven. My father was an information dispenser. My mother was really uptight. I learned nothing from her because she could hardly spit anything out."

What many parents do spit out is a collection of simple facts their sons and daughters learned in seventh-grade health class. They rarely give their children any information on subjects which the schools, fearful of controversy, have failed to cover. Yet these very subjects—birth control, premarital sex, the advantages and disadvantages of living together, and sexual techniques—are what young people want and need to discuss.

When she was fifteen, the Alice in *Go Ask Alice* wished she could talk with her mother about sex and expressed these wishes in her diary. "I wonder if when she was my age she worried about boys not liking her and girls being only part-time friends. I wonder if boys were as oversexed in those days as they are now. None of my friends ever go all the way, but I guess a lot of the girls at school do. I wish I could talk to my mother about things like this because I don't really believe a lot of the kids know what they're talking about, at least I can't believe all the stuff they tell me."

Notice that Alice asked no biological questions. She needed *personal* feedback. She needed to hear her mother speak about her own memories of growing up, her own encounters with boys when she was in high school, and her feelings about them now. The most serious questions about sex always focus on feelings, peer pressure, and the struggle to decide what is right.

Alice never did have that talk with her mother. Within months of that entry in her diary, it was too late, and she no longer cared about having such a talk. The wishes she expressed are shared by many teenagers, male and female; that is why it is a mistake for you to assume that once your children have reached their mid to late teens, speaking about sex will be useless. A respected columnist once told an inquiring mother that talking to a seventeen-year-old about sex would be like trying to give a fish a bath. She was wrong: such a talk can be of immense and lasting value to both parent and teenager.

An eighteen-year-old whose parents have never mentioned sex to her echoes many of Alice's feelings. "I would like to have had both my parents talk with me about sex when I was fifteen. That was when I was hassling with guys trying to get me to go to bed with them. When I was thirteen or fourteen I started sneaking around so I could go out with guys, and if my parents had talked with me then too, we might have trusted each other a little more. They could have seen where I stood."

What would she have wanted to hear from her parents? "I've always wondered, when they were my age, how they felt and what they did. How their friends felt. What it was like when they first met, and how they feel about me now. I would like to have been really open with them, and had them be really open with me. . ."

She looked wistful and said she would still like to have that talk, but felt sure it would never happen. She is the oldest child in an intelligent family, but as in so many families, both parents and children send each other non-verbal signals which say, "Let's not speak about sex."

The problem with not talking is that for virtually every teenager, the big question about sex is not whether; instead,

## THE QUESTION IS WHEN

When is sex permissible? When is it good? When is it harmful? Parents must face these questions and answer them.

The Gallup Poll shows that adult approval of premarital sex is up from thirty-two percent in 1969 to fifty-two percent in 1973. Nevertheless, I suspect that most parents with teenagers remain in the opposed category, and the kids know it. Even so, at least one of every four teenagers and possibly as many as two of every four have had intercourse. These are national figures; they apply to Mobile and Peoria just as surely as they do to New York and San Francisco.*

A group of psychiatrists has argued that, depending on the maturity of a given adolescent couple, kids in their late teens should feel free to have sex. I have trouble with this point of view because I know dozens of teenagers who are amazingly mature, intelligent, responsible people—except when it comes to sex. And how could they be otherwise? Who has bothered to give them straightforward advice and information? Not the schools. Not the churches. Not the media. And not many parents.

The only fair measure of the impact of intercourse during high school would be a study of case after case, comparing couples who have had intercourse and couples who are virgins. My own conclusions are not scientific, but I do believe that ideally no high school student should have intercourse. My reasons are essentially practical ones.

First and most obviously, the girl can get pregnant. Although we have a growing number of free clinics which offer confidential birth control services to teenagers, girls still get pregnant. A school survey

---

* Figures slightly higher than one in four are indicated by M. Zelnik and J.F. Kanter in a study available through the U.S. Government Printing Office. Figures slightly higher than two in four are indicated in a study entitled *Adolescent Sexuality in Contemporary America* by Robert C. Sorensen, World Publishing Company, 1973.

in wealthy Marin County, California, gives us a hint at the reason why.

Forty percent of the high school students in Marin have had intercourse, but only half of them bothered to use any form of contraceptive, even though ninety-nine percent of these same kids consider themselves well informed about birth control! They explain that "sex seems less immoral when it happens spontaneously," when one is carried away by the passions of the moment. Of course, if they were more candid, they would admit that the "spontaneous" moment is often the result of weeks of careful planning, including clever forethought about place, privacy, occasion, and the procurement of booze. To preserve the image of spontaneity, the planning must be discreet; and there is nothing discreet about a condom.

While a growing number of teenagers are choosing to have intercourse, very few of them really make an honest decision. They prefer to let it happen if it is going to happen, and the result is often an unwanted pregnancy. There is truth in the ironic contrast between the wife who tries for years to get pregnant without success and the teenage girl who takes a chance and gets pregnant the very first time. In 1972 there were half a million single teenage girls in this country who got pregnant. They are my number one reason for waiting.

Second, high school students rarely have the opportunity to give sex its proper due. In the words of one sixteen-year-old girl, "It's depressing to think how many kids ball under slimy conditions and then feel so disgusted about it later. Like balling when you're drunk or stoned, for instance."

Honest love-making deserves much better than that. When we lose too many moments that should have been both rare and good, we lose life itself. Most teenagers do believe it's wrong to have sex when they are drunk or stoned, but intercourse does often happen under precisely those circumstances. For many girls and some boys, the aftertaste is one of guilt and self-betrayal.

The guilt is a third reason for waiting. Even if we could all accept Hemingway's loose moral code ("what is moral is what you feel good after and what is immoral is what you feel bad after"), we would have to say that many sexual episodes are immoral—even by that standard. Girls often feel a combination of embarrassment, sorrow, and disappointment after their first experience with intercourse. They also remember feeling afraid. And I'm not talking about girls in Victorian England or American girls in the fifties, I'm talking about now. These days even boys are getting in touch with a sense of loss when sex is pursued on a dishonest basis.

Guilt is a cancer of the soul. It eats away from the inside, and none of us can stand much of it. Young people are idealistic, they believe in love and friendship much more than they believe in sex, and so when sex begins to dominate a romance it very often falls apart. A breakup between people who have risked a great deal with each other is hard to absorb at any age; it is particularly hard when we are either very young or very old.

And those are my reasons for believing no high school student should have intercourse. I know the chances are that most young people will disagree with my conclusion. Love is often all passion and no perspective or it wouldn't be love. My rational arguments pale against the enchanting powers of moonlight, soft words, and growing love. The heart often wins the battle between head and heart, and thank God it does! What a dull planet we would have if dry reason dictated all our major decisions.

So despite my pragmatic reasons for abstention, it is only fair to say that age does of course make a difference. A thirteen-year-old is not the same as a nineteen-year-old, even though they may look and act remarkably the same. We are breeding quite a large number of very mature fourteen-year-olds these days, but none of them are quite as mature as they would like the world to think. I believe that younger teenagers in particular should allow the mysteries of sex to remain mysteries a while longer. If you agree, then counsel the wisdom of waiting, should you get the chance. Say it gently and with humor, and then hope that although he and she are willing and able, perhaps they won't be quite as ready and won't quite have the nerve.

## LEARNED HELPLESSNESS

Most high school girls believe that intercourse and love go together. If they have sex at all, it is usually with a boy they love.

Their relationship will either endure or collapse as time goes by, but while it lasts the girl and often the boy as well are in love.

A few girls who have an early experience with intercourse may then go to a series of casual episodes because they pretend they can't help themselves. They still believe that love and sex go together, and like most of us they understand the meaning of the word "used." If they feel a new boyfriend is pushing too hard, they may warn him, "You better not use me." But a week or a month later they admit to a friend or to a counselor, "I was used."

A young girl caught in this pattern dislikes herself because other people, especially her parents, seem to dislike her. Almost everything she says about herself and about life in general is negative, and her obsessive despair feeds on itself, growing with time into ever more despondent moods. She is overwhelmed if she finds a friend, particularly a male friend, who likes her "for herself," but rarely meets anyone like that because she has come to suspect everyone. She believes that one has to perform in order to get approval, and she is often right about this if you look at the people around her. As one girl said, "If I want my parents to like me I have to do something they want like clean up my room, get a good grade, dress up, things like that. The guys I go out with are the same way. If I don't ball them, they forget me."

A person like this is caught in the pre-suicidal trap I described earlier, the trap research psychologists call "learned helplessness." No effort permits escape from the pain. Despair takes over, an overwhelming feeling that "no matter what I do, it's no use, my life won't change." Unfortunately, some parents with promiscuous daughters contribute to this feeling of helplessness in a thoughtless moment of rage: "You're no better than a common whore!" Inside herself that girl says, "They're right." And she goes on proving it.

If help comes, it comes because the girl makes a suicide attempt, or because she gets pregnant and meets a good counselor, or because she uses enough drugs to gain an adult's notice. She *can* change. The process of teaching a person a new perspective on life takes time and patience, but the principles involved are really very simple. A detailed illustration of those principles in action is included in the section on sex in Chapter 2.

## GETTING PREGNANT

You may be conservative, liberal, or undecided about the morality of sex outside of marriage, but if your teenage daughter gets pregnant, you are simply a parent with a child—most probably a badly frightened child—who needs your help. Moralizing will be redundant; your daughter, even if her outward pose is one of defiance, will already have given herself a dozen scoldings harsher than any you could give her.

In 1973, more than 705,000 unmarried girls between fifteen and nineteen got pregnant. More than half of those girls ended their pregnancy in abortion. One-quarter of them chose to have their babies, a trend that is rising among white, middle-class teenage girls. The other girls in the 1973 survey either got married or lost their babies in a miscarriage. It is important to note that these figures do not include the girls under age fifteen who got pregnant that year; if they did, the total number of unmarried pregnancies in 1973 would be close to 900,000.[*]

Do you want your daughter to come to you if she gets pregnant? Many girls have secret abortions and never tell their parents about what they have just gone through. Many others, afraid to say anything to their parents, pretend the pregnancy is a dream and refuse to see a doctor as the months go by, endangering their own health as well as the child's. They will talk with their parents only when forced to do so by the undeniable evidence of a growing abdomen. This fear of parental reaction is particularly true in white middle- and upper–class suburbs where too many parents have made it clear to their daughters that an unwanted pregnancy is the one disgrace they never want to hear about. Secret abortions are extremely high in the suburbs for precisely this reason.

Black girls are more likely to go to their parents because the reality of unwanted pregnancy is faced more openly by most black

[*] From the *Journal of Clinical Child Psychology*, Fall-Winter 1974, in an article entitled "Out-of-Wedlock Pregnancy among American Teenagers" by Gene Vadies and Richard Pomeroy.

parents. "If it ever happens to you, Patricia, I don't want you going off someplace by yourself, you hear me? I want you coming straight to me, and that's the truth!" White parents would do well to borrow a share of this black candor.

All girls wonder how their parents will react. One girl who wants to have her baby is afraid her parents will force her to get an abortion to avoid family disgrace, and she hides her pregnancy not because she is ashamed but so she can give her baby enough time to develop to the point when an abortion will be legally impossible. Another girl keeps her pregnancy secret for the opposite reason: she is afraid her parents will refuse to allow an abortion. She raises money on her own and, one day when her parents think she is shopping or visiting a friend, she goes to a women's clinic and gets an abortion. It can be done that quickly. Both of these girls are afraid that you, as a parent, will condemn them. They are especially fearful of what their fathers will think.

A pregnant girl needs her parents' support, and she needs sound advice from an outside source, from someone she knows is objective. She should be given all the alternatives that are open to her and understand the possible consequences of each alternative. Looked at objectively, none of the choices are appealing.

The medical consequences of an early pregnancy can be extremely serious. Pregnancy for girls seventeen and younger involves abnormal risks for the baby; premature births, stillbirths, and infant mortality in the first year after birth are all more likely when the mother is a teenager. These risks are especially high for mothers fifteen and younger because at that age the girl's own life is also at stake. Prematurity is linked to epilepsy, cerebral palsy, mental retardation, and increased risk of deafness and blindness. These risks can be minimized even for young girls if they will get prompt and proper prenatal care; but if a girl is obsessed by guilt and fear and thus hides her pregnancy until the fourth or fifth month, she escalates all of these dangers enormously.

The social consequences of teenage pregnancy are equally distressing as the possible physical risks. Having a baby out of wedlock usually causes a sad turning point in a young mother's life. Her baby is not an adventure but a sentence. She probably will have to drop out of school, and will probably fail to find good-paying work.

She may marry a man she would not have chosen under other circumstances. The number of "early marriages" is declining, but there are still more than 100,000 of them every year. Twice that many young girls decide against a forced marriage and have their babies as single women.

Martha is a girl who had a baby four years ago. She is tall and pixie-like with unnaturally hollow blue eyes. She lives in a two-bedroom apartment with her son, Mark. Mark's father lived with them for slightly over a year and then left for good. He contributes nothing to his son's needs, and Martha neither knows nor cares where he is. She has a few friends, mostly younger than she, who come to her apartment because it is a safe place to get stoned. She has had five brief, trivial and punishing affairs with men over the past two years; three of the men were married. There are hundreds of thousands of Marthas. And Marks.

No girl has to live a life like that. If you have ever thought about adopting an infant, then you know the waiting lists are like the lines at the most popular attraction in Disneyland. Martha was following a current trend among young, unwed mothers. She kept Mark because he was hers, he had been with her for nine months already, she had struggled with the pain that gave him life. It was too impossibly unnatural for her to go through all of that and then not even look at him on the day after he was born. It is easy to see her now and say that she was irrational then, but how hard it is to be Martha, to make a rational decision about your newborn child.

The most significant trend in 1975, a trend likely to continue, is toward abortion. At least 200,000 teenage girls had abortions in 1972; only half of them were legal. By 1973 close to 400,000 teenagers had abortions, and most of them were legal. Those numbers went up another twenty-five percent in 1974 and may have climbed still more in 1975.

Most of the teenage girls who choose to have abortions deal quite well with the physical and emotional traumas they endure. Their basic reaction after the abortion is relief—a tremendous psychological and emotional strain is suddenly gone. A young woman of sixteen or seventeen has lived for several weeks with the fear that she might be pregnant, she has gone to a strange clinic where a strange doctor told her it was true, she has wondered whether to tell her parents and, if she has kept it a secret from them, has had to find some way to raise the money for an abortion. If she allowed herself to think about it, she has been through a struggle with the moral implications of her decision. Most of the girls who get abortions feel sure they are doing the right thing, and all good abortion clinics have skilled counselors on the staff.

Even so, a few girls feel forced into an abortion they don't want. Lisa, now seventeen, felt razor-sharp pains during her abortion one year ago, even though the doctor used an aspiration device which eliminates any need to scrape the uterus. Lisa had kept her pregnancy a total secret, even from her boyfriend. Her mother is an image-conscious socialite, so Lisa was reluctant to tell her anything. Lisa's maternal instinct was strong, she loved her boyfriend, and in her heart she wanted to have the baby. But her fear of her mother's reaction won out. Later on she also admitted that she didn't want her boyfriend to feel trapped. So she had the abortion and her body responded reflexively to prevent it. She never talks about that experience anymore, but has never forgiven herself for it.

What can you do to help if a daughter of yours gets pregnant? The decision to have the baby and keep it, to have the baby and give it up for adoption, or to have an abortion is finally a decision which belongs to the girl. Help her sort through all of these alternatives if you are lucky enough to have her come to you for help, and then support her decision—or at least allow her decision—even if it violates your own personal view. She will live with it much longer than you will.

## PARENTAL DISTRUST

A mother watched her beautiful young daughter leave the house with her very first date, a most striking young man. As they drove off the mother exclaimed, "My God, they both look so physical!" The kids were fifteen. A comment like that is natural and innocent; however, some parents develop an abiding distrust, a distrust which focuses on daughters and on the boys who take out daughters, but not on sons. One of the worst results of this distrust is that it can make a girl feel cheap.

Betsy went out with Tim for almost a year. They had a strong relationship emotionally and physically, and Tim wanted to make love. Betsy was opposed. One night Tim made her feel guilty for "holding out" on him. He said he felt they should break up, and he accused Betsy of causing the break by insisting on her "puritanical view of sex." Betsy went home that night feeling alone and vulnerable. She had spent an extra hour trying to make Tim see things her way, so she was late when she unlocked the front door and walked into the living room.

Her father was up, sitting in his chair looking totally bored by the late movie on television. The extra hour of waiting had fed his suspicious nature; he wanted to know why Betsy had been out so late.

"I just had some things to talk over with Tim."

"Was that what you were doing—talking?"

"Yes. And I don't want to argue about it. If you don't believe me, I can't help it."

"I didn't sit here waiting until two in the morning just to listen to your snotty remarks."

Holding her with his gaze, Betsy's father delivered an angry speech that ended with "You better watch yourself, young lady, or soon you'll be no better than the hookers down on Hennepin Avenue!" He stomped off to bed and left his daughter in tears.

An unusual incident? Not at all. And by some ironic twist of fate, the girls who struggle hardest with their feelings, the girls who want to be certain that sex is as beautiful for them as it can possibly be, are often the girls whose parents confront them in a suspicious moment of anger and call them whores. Some girls are strong enough to let the word go by, but all of them are stung by that kind of accusation and many end up deciding that it might be true.

Another common incident caused by parental distrust can have serious consequences. Diane and Gary dated for almost two years. She was president of the senior class at her high school and an honor roll student. He was an equally popular school athlete. They went to Diane's house one afternoon after school, found no one at home, had a snack and walked to the rear of the one-story house where Diane shared a room with her younger sister. Less than an hour later her parents came home and caught them, fully clothed, lying on Diane's bed.

Parents usually either overreact or underreact in this kind of situation. They explode and throw the boy out of the house, or they walk away and try to pretend that nothing untoward had happened. Diane's father threw Gary out of the house, and Diane was reminded of the incident for weeks. She felt that her parents had made their minds up that she was a reincarnation of Hester Prynne. After trying several times to get her parents to drop the issue, Diane left home. She moved in with a girl friend, threw herself into her school work, and turned down dates.

After graduation that year she began seeing an extremely gentle young man. Her feelings for him were genuinely warm and open, yet she reacted with an involuntary shudder whenever he touched her. She slowly got over the shudder but couldn't stand any intimate touching or kissing.

Teenagers need good reactions from you in crisis situations, honest reactions; they need to know that you are leveling with them. If Diane's parents had ignored the bedroom incident, she would have wondered what they really thought and she might have guilted herself even more than she actually did. As it was, her parents went in the opposite direction and guilted her into a state of frigidity that may take years to overcome. It is always hard to react perfectly in a crisis, but it is always possible to react well. All you need is the determination to give yourself enough time to consider your response, to taste the words before you say them.

Most parents never have to deal with the reality of their kids' sex lives. Your sons and daughters are likely to mature, date, make out, fall in and out of love, stay out too late, go steady, and leave home for job or college, all without incident. Decisions about love-making will have been made without asking for your words of wisdom. The outcome of those private decisions will remain, in most cases, private—which is just as it should be.

So your decision is: to what extent do I want to intrude myself into that whole process, speak my mind, and either get out or leave myself open for future talks? I believe most teenagers wish they could have at least one honest talk about sex with their parents. It is often a buried wish, unexpressed and unfulfilled, but if you feel you'd like to make an effort toward talking, your first question may be:

## HOW DO I BRING IT UP?

Maybe you never should. Some parents simply do not want to talk about sex with their children; they feel very uncomfortable with the idea, and they may sense a warning within themselves—a signal that their obvious discomfort can do their children more harm than good. If you have this feeling yourself, don't try to talk with your kids.

Our feelings about sex are based on the personal experiences we have had. If your experiences have been largely frustrating and unfulfilling, the worst thing you could do would be to pass these feelings along to your children. You may have done so already without saying a word. Jane's mother, for example, is a man-hater. She is forty-three, divorced, and working on her ninth lover in six years. She seems to deliberately choose men who mistreat her, who drink too much as her ex-husband did, and who use her sexually. It is her way of proving to herself and the world that all men are bastards. She has never talked with her daughter about sex, but her dreary script is not lost on Jane, who, at eighteen, has never let a boy touch her intimately. Her suspicion of men and her distrust of herself are inherited non-verbally from her mother. Many teenagers and adults have taken distorted sexual cues from their parents, a sad progression in which the hangups of the parents are visited upon their children from generation to generation.

A more common problem is the sometimes subtle, sometimes blatant sexual competition that some parents get into with their teenage kids. If I am forty-five when my kids reach their teens, I am on a sexual decline just as my son is becoming a virile young stud. A mother watches her daughters develop long, slender legs and firm breasts and knows that, personally, the days of looking like that are gone forever. The point, for both mother and father, is that those days *are* gone. If you have accepted that fact and have gone to better things, you're in good shape. But some parents refuse to grow old gracefully. Father goes mod at forty-five, lets his hair grow a bit, and stops acting his age around younger women. Mother puts on a short skirt, high boots, and a tight sweater—all from her daughter's wardrobe if she can manage it. If you see yourself mirrored here, don't try talking with your kids about sex. You need to settle some issues for yourself first.

These problems are not your problems? Then back to the original question: "How do I bring it up?" Begin by getting in touch with the fact that you have already brought it up, non-verbally, in everything you and your spouse have done over the years. Your kids have a message from you now, whether you realize it or not. Without saying a word you have shown them how you feel about touching, how you feel about nakedness, how you feel about intimacy—how you feel about sex. If sex is accepted as a natural and marvelous part of life by you and your spouse, this attitude will have filtered down through your family and you won't have to worry about how to bring up the subject. The kids will automatically come to you when they need you.

I don't mean to dodge the question or to talk only about ideal worlds. The next best answer to "How do I bring it up?" is to set the stage so your children will have every possible opportunity to bring it up themselves, no matter what non-verbal messages you've given them. Many kids hate to be sat down and talked to when they haven't initiated the discussion, no matter what the subject is, so your goal may be to get them to ask.

You can be sure of one thing: your young teenager is thinking about sex most of his waking hours even if his outward pose is one of casual nonchalance toward the opposite sex. One way to open up dialogue is to give him a book. There are lots of good books about sex these days, and you'll find them geared to every age level. The type of book you choose will say something about the level you think your teenager has reached, and his response (e.g., "I already knew that stuff," or "I've been too busy to read it") will say something more.

When you hand over the book (don't make a big deal out of it), you can say, "I've read this book and I think it's really good. See what you think." Or, "I liked most of this and I disagreed with some of it. See what you think." You have issued a simple invitation, an invitation that can be refused but may be accepted. A week later you might ask, "What did you think of the book?" Don't be discouraged if he says, "What book?" If you have an aggressive style, there's nothing wrong with asking a leading question like "What did you think of the section on premarital sex?" Of course you can say nothing at all, figuring that it's his move to make if he cares to. The point is that you have provided an opening for discussion.

Get away from the idea that a talk about sex must be conducted in quiet voices off in a private room. Kitchen table discussions are often the best kind, with your other children listening in and contributing if they are so inclined. Try to make your family's attitude toward sex open enough so your kids will feel free to ask questions while you're fixing dinner or changing the oil in the car. At the same time, they should know you're available for a private talk if that's what they need.

The best way to create an open family attitude toward talking about sex is to start young. If you are honest with your six-year-old about where babies come from, he is more likely to bring honest questions to you when he is twelve. You can overdo it, of course. There is an old joke about six-year-old Johnny who comes home from school one afternoon and asks, "Mommy, where did I come from?" His mother thinks Johnny is too young to be hearing the facts of life, but she doesn't want him to rely on the kind of information his schoolmates are likely to give him. So she decides to tell all. When she has finished with a truly admirable account of the human reproductive process, little Johnny says, "Well, I just wondered where I came from. Suzie Smith told me she came from St. Louis." Small children don't need the whole story from you, but when they show an interest make a small beginning.

If you're one of the millions of parents who didn't start this way, just do your best at this later date to provide opportunities for question and discussion. For example, you can simply acknowledge your teenager's sexuality. As your daughter matures, compliment the way she looks. Even a comment like "You really look sexy tonight" is appropriate if it isn't overused. And remember, a girl today can look very appealing, at least to her peers, in faded jeans and an old work shirt. Tell your son how good he looks as he leaves to pick up a date, but don't say, "That Kathy you've been taking out really has a great figure, doesn't she!" And don't make cracks to your daughter like "Jim seems to have fallen for you," or "Isn't it nice that Jim wants to take you out again!" Those comments sound pushy to a teenager even when you mean them only as a sincere expression of interest. When you acknowledge naturally developing sexuality without pushing it on your teenager, you build a foundation for honest talking about sex.

If you draw no response from offered books, compliments, or any other efforts to open up discussion, you will hardly be shirking duty if you drop the whole idea of a talk. The only other choice is to come right out and arrange one: "I want to get together with you this evening and have a talk about sex." Nothing wrong with that approach; after all, it is the most common one. The guidelines that follow are designed to help make any talk with your teenagers, whether initiated by you or by them, as profitable as possible.

### 1. Start by admitting your anxiety.

Talking about sex is a very anxiety-producing thing to do in our culture, especially when you are trying to talk with your own children. So you feel nervous? You know that's normal. And the best way to disarm your anxious feelings is to bring them out into the open. You may be talking sex with your teenager for the first time, and in that case it would be appropriate to say, "I've never done this before—it's a new thing for me—and I'm a little nervous. Are you feeling the same way?" You can't go wrong when you start with the actual feelings you're having at the moment, and since those feelings are likely to be anxious, nervous ones, you'll set a tone of honesty and candor by talking about them before you go on to anything else.

### 2. Don't try to be an expert.

The sexual revolution has made some parents wonder whether their kids know more than they do about sex. Asked whether he has talked with his fourteen-year-old son about sex, a typical father might say, "Jesus, he knows more now than I knew at nineteen!" And he's wondering whether the little guy already knows more than he knows now! If he does, so what? You are not Masters and Johnson. Your job is not to bring your kid up-to-date on the latest sexual techniques. Instead, prepare yourself by trying to get in touch with your own teenage years. For half an hour, be fourteen years old again. Where were you then? What sexual feelings did you have then? Did you have a crush on someone? Who? Let yourself fall back into that time and place.

Now think: what did your parents say to you about sex? What would you have liked to hear from them? Did only one of them speak with you about sex? Would you have liked to have a talk with the parent who didn't speak with you? What were your feelings when you first went out with someone? Who took the lead physically? What physical things were okay and what was not? How did you make those decisions? What did you want to do?

The answers to those questions are a large part of what your kid would like to hear you talk about. You don't have to be an expert on sex; all you need is willingness to search your memory and reminisce out loud.

### 3. Don't make agreement your goal.

The purpose of any parent-teenager discussion is to share information, ideas, and feelings, not to achieve agreement on every issue. Make sure your kids know that agreement is less important to you than understanding. Most kids tell their parents only what they think they can take passively in order to avoid an argument about sex. They will let you think they agree with everything you say when, in fact, their personal opinions are radically different from yours.

### 4. Team up with your spouse.

Father-daughter and mother-son talks are good, just as father-son and mother-daughter talks are, and if you and your spouse have got it together, you should plan one three-way discussion with each of your kids. In mid-adolescence at the latest, young people begin to see you not just as father and mother but as husband and wife, as two people with a relationship that is defined by much more than parenthood. Try to guess how your teenagers see you as a couple. Do you display your affection openly or do you touch and kiss only behind closed doors? If you have a happy sex life, how might your teenagers guess it? What have you said to them in so many words about sex? Do they know how you feel about premarital sex? about sexual pleasure? about petting?

Any preparation for a three-way discussion involves some soul-searching with your spouse. What differences of opinion do you have? Do you feel the same way about premarital intercourse? Are your feelings about your son's sex life different from your feelings about your daughter's sex life? If so, which of you has what feeling? What do you both feel about young people living together before marriage? Whatever you do, don't try to plan a united front. Your teenagers will have heard a dozen different opinions so it will not hurt them to learn that their parents are individuals, that two adults can love each other without seeing life in precisely the same terms. Your discussion will be more helpful and more interesting if you leave in the rough spots.

How do you begin? Kids are fascinated by the details of their parents' early romance. How did you meet? What did you think of each other at first? Who suggested meeting again after your first encounter? When did you start to get serious? How long did it take before your first kiss? What did you see in each other that made you decide to get married? If you haven't already talked about those days in casual conversations with your children, be sure to include them in your three-way discussion. When you start from such an interesting point, the rest of the discussion will take care of itself.

Am I asking you to say things out loud to your children that you have never said out loud to each other? If so, it is still true that

### 5. A general discussion is better than nothing.

Some of us, in spite of our best intentions, wind up talking about sex as if we were discussing the national economy. All of our comments stay on an impersonal, intellectual level even when we might like to get more into our feelings. This is a normal, protective maneuver we all use. Our feeling is that it's okay to talk about sex in general or about what other people are doing but not about what we did last Saturday night! Some parents even have a mutual pact with their teenagers, an unspoken vow of silence. As one girl explained, "Around my house, I don't say that balling is right and my parents don't say that balling is wrong." If feelings are strong on both sides, it is probably better to leave a pact like that just as it is.

Having a good sex talk is actually harder than having a good sex life. So don't feel badly if your talk stays in the clouds; you're still way ahead of the crowd just by giving it a try.

### 6. Don't jump to conclusions.

Trust, once again, is an essential prerequisite for a good talk. If you are asked a frank question or two, consider yourself lucky, and remember this story.

Leslie asked her mother whether birth control pills are dangerous. She got an objective answer, but her mother was left with the nagging suspicion that Leslie might be planning to go on the pill. Why else would she ask a question like that? You may often be tempted to assume that an innocent question, asked on Monday afternoon, is really a plan of action for Saturday night.

Leslie's mother worried for a month and then did something she had promised herself she would never do; she searched her daughter's purse and her bureau drawers. Although she found nothing, she still wondered and looked suspiciously at Leslie's handsome new boyfriend. Another month passed, and one Friday night before Leslie went out her mother said, "Don't stay out half the night playing around with Michael." The words came out with a dirty undertone that was not fully intended.

Leslie was deeply hurt by that remark. It made her mad, but it also made her feel cheap. Although her question about the pill had been entirely innocent, she would never know that it was the reason for her mother's comment.

The lesson is obvious. Whatever you are asked, whether it is asked in a planned discussion or comes as a casual question out of the blue over milk and cookies, try to give an honest answer. Never say, "Why do you want to know?" And if you get a question that stumps you, promise to help find the answer. You'll be glad your kids got it from you.

## 7. If nothing else, talk to your sons.

Girls who sleep around are called promiscuous. Promiscuity means frequent sex relations without much affection. Relatively few girls are ever promiscuous.

Boys who sleep around are called studs. Our society still celebrates the stud. Confessed male virgins are now an endangered species because to be male, eighteen, and a virgin is to feel vaguely inadequate, as if you have shirked your duty.

Fathers rarely advocate celibacy for their high-school-age sons; mostly they say nothing at all. Meanwhile, Madison Avenue uses the stud to sell everything from cars to cigarettes. Films glorify his macho spasms. Every young man gets the message that it's important to score, both on the field and in the bed. The chastity belt was invented for women, after all, not men, and locker-room morality is the same as always. If you can get away with it, if you can be discreet about it—more power to you, son.

If anything, male arrogance is more brazen than ever. This is particularly true when a boy is with a girl he knows, according to his friend, is no longer a virgin. He expects to be in bed with her if he spends a certain amount of time with her, and may consider one night quite enough time. He will be seriously insulted if she says no, and will lash out at her if he senses her vulnerability. His message is "Unless you give me what I want—and what *you* really want, too, if you'd just admit it—then I'm going to make you feel like hell. So why not let me have it? It won't make any difference to you anyway."

The double standard was invented by men for the benefit of men. It is a despicably immoral conspiracy, alive and well and living today in America despite women's liberation. It says that free love is okay for boys but not for girls. Young girls are brainwashed—by parents! —into believing that boys are unable to control their sex drive. The girl, not the boy, is made responsible for drawing the line during a petting session. The boy is expected to go as far as he can. Girls wind up believing that it's natural for boys to paw them and that "the guys really can't help it." When things "get out of control," the girl gets the blame. She is blamed by her parents, by society, and by herself.

The truth is that males of any age can and should control their sexual behavior. Parents might help modify male behavior by refusing to give their sons unwritten approval for their sexual exploits. Stop sending double messages: "Go to it!" to your sons and "Be careful!" to your daughters. Fathers, you can try talking to your sons about some of those male qualities that don't depend on sexual prowess; mothers, you can tell your sons what a girl feels like when she is being pressured or mauled. On the positive side, you can share with your sons what a girl likes, including what you liked in boys when you were a girl going through school. Both parents can let sons know how thoroughly you deplore deceit and game-playing in any area of life. Talk about the deeper meanings of romance, about the respect and honesty that make it good.

.Very few parents ever instruct their teenagers about birth control, and those who do usually go over the details with their daughters, not with their sons. Remind your son that he must share the responsibility for preventing pregnancy should he make love to a girl. Once you have tried to teach him to respect the rights and feelings of the girls he dates, show him you also can understand that he may have a romance in which sex seems right and natural both to him and his girl. You may not approve, but if you tell him that you know such a moment may come, you will leave yourself open for future talks and you will have let him know that if he ever needs help in a crisis, you will be there.

A few young men are working out a new sexual morality for themselves. "I just can't get into balling a girl I don't love," says one. "I'm all for hustling chicks because I really like talking with them, but I can't see playing lots of games to get them into bed. For some guys, sex is a big ego thing. I'd like to make love with a girl who loves me, but you don't run into girls who love you every day, and I'm not going to go out with a chick just to see if I can ball her. I don't need it that bad."

## THE FUTURE

Who knows, virginity may come back into style. It's just about the only sexual novelty left. We may even see a counterrevolution of values led by the children of aging radicals, although at the moment we have a growing trend toward more sex apart from marriage and sex at much earlier ages. The number of new teenage patients being seen at Planned Parenthood clinics across the country increased 744% between 1966 and 1972, and that doesn't count the teenagers who go to the independent free clinics. There is not just more candid talking about sex by young people these days, there is more action as well.

Maybe young people are just being more clear-eyed about sex than we were. When petting gets heavy enough, virginity becomes a physical technicality rather than a moral reality. For some kids, it has seemed more honest to go ahead and make love. If you are sorely distressed by all this, you may find some comfort in these words, spoken by an old man to a young man in John Fowles' novel *The Magus:*

"You young people can lend your bodies now, play with them, give them as we could not. But remember that you have paid a price: that of a world rich in mystery and delicate emotion. It is not only species of animal that die out. But whole species of feeling. And if you are wise you will never pity the past for what it did not know."

# 8

## Drugs

The police officer noticed a small group of kids, growing larger by the minute, gathering in the early evening shadows down by the lake. He walked over to check them out; it was a Saturday in the spring of 1972. When he got close he could see the sixteen-gallon keg and he knew that a majority of the crowd was underage, though not by much. When they spotted him, the owners of the keg looked apprehensive.

"Planning a little party?" asked the officer in a friendly tone.

"Sure," said one of the kids. "Want a beer?"

The officer smiled. "No, thanks. You guys got any junior high kids in this crowd?"

"Nah, we don't let them come around. They just ruin things for everyone."

"Okay, listen: you keep this party down here in the park, away from the people in town, and I'll leave you alone. But if you come up into the streets, I'll bust you. Is that clear?"

"We got everything we need right down here," said a voice from the shadows.

"Don't worry, Jim," said the long-haired muscular kid next to the keg. "We appreciate what you're doin', and we won't blow it."

Jim nodded a farewell and walked the two blocks back up into town to continue his evening rounds.

More than three hundred high school and college-age young people were in the park that night for the first of a series of whooping Saturday-night keg parties. Officer Jim's peace treaty took on the force of a liquor license in the minds of teenagers for miles around;

they stayed in the park, minded their own business, and got falling-down drunk.

The bargain might have worked if it hadn't been for the junior high kids. On the third Saturday, after the party started, dozens of them swooped into the park. They conned beers, combined the beer with bourbon they had stolen from home, and charged up into town like the dregs from the army of Attila the Hun. They yowled through the streets in small bunches, knocking over trash cans, breaking radio antenna off cars, and shouting, "Ooga booga!" at old ladies walking into Woolworth's.

Public pressure soon forced the police to patrol the park in an effort to stop the drinking. But every cop knew the juvenile courts wanted nothing to do with three hundred kids charged with drinking. The court didn't even want to process the kids who were charged with possession of marijuana. There were simply too many cases for the judges to handle.

To understand why officer Jim tried his bargain in the first place, you have to remember the mood in thousands of towns across America in 1972. Like many small towns, Jim's town had its share of small-time drugs: marijuana, hashish, speed, downers, and LSD. The police had utterly failed to catch any of the major dealers, all of whom were young people. Drugs had scared most adults so badly that when a group of kids were seen drinking beer, the adults practically broke into applause. Here was something they knew, a return to the Old Way!

When Jim walked down to the lake that Saturday evening to check out the crowd, he recognized ten or twelve kids who had been spending most of their time stoned on marijuana or something heavier. There was no smell of pot in the air that night, only the odor of the freshly tapped keg. He wondered if the drug tide might be turning at last. If so, why not encourage the change? "If these freaks really want to drink beer, I say let 'em do it—it's a helluva big improvement over what they've *been* doing!"

Jim's attitude was shared by many parents who, in the presence of their teenagers, tacitly approved of drinking and condemned the use of other drugs. By 1973 booze was back on top in many high schools—the kids had gotten the message. Other drugs were still around, marijuana and hash in particular, but times were definitely changing.

One young man just out of high school explained it this way: "I was really into smoking dope, I just really dug being stoned all the time. I still enjoy getting stoned, but now I think there's a time and a place. Lately I'm using a lot more alcohol. When I'm stoned and I try to do something physical like play baseball, I just can't do it. But I can when I'm drinking beer. If I want to sit around at a party and talk to a lot of people, I can't get stoned because if I do, I'm useless—I'm so out of it I can't talk to anybody. Somebody comes walkin' up to me and says, 'How're you doin'?' And all I can say is 'Stoned, man, stoned.'

"That used to be far out about three years ago when you'd go to a party and everybody would be sittin' around just lookin' at each other. All anybody said all night long was 'Stoned, man, stoned.' But alcohol loosens people up. Everybody gets a little rowdy and everybody likes to stand around and bullshit with each other and do active things. I think that's a lot of the reason why people are smoking dope less and drinking more."

And he is right, but the police are still not sure how to react. It was serious business in 1968 to be arrested for even a minuscule amount of marijuana. Three years later, many juvenile officers were letting kids go with a warning the first and second times they were caught with an ounce or less. The juvenile courts had gotten sick of simple possession charges because too many of the arrested kids were intelligent, functional people who didn't belong in court. In addition, new studies refuted the worst claims that had been made about marijuana, and some experts were ready to say that it was less dangerous than smoking ordinary cigarettes. But adults remained uncomfortable with marijuana and welcomed the apparent return to beer. The welcome was short-lived; they had forgotten how loud three hundred kids drunk can be. The police were ordered to begin patrolling the old watering places again, and the kids who had been drinking in relative peace while all the heat was on the dope crowd were suddenly looking at uniforms before they had even tapped their kegs or tossed their pop tops.

The renewed popularity of alcohol among young people is nothing to celebrate. According to the National Institute on Alcohol Abuse and Alcoholism, 1.3 million kids between the ages of twelve and seventeen have serious drinking problems. Television and the slick magazines have called attention to the rising problem of teen-age alcoholism—we now have twelve-year-old kids in this country who are alcoholics!

Alcohol is a drug, too, and the word "drug" in this chapter is meant to include alcohol right along with the street drugs. We have begun an extremely dangerous period in our social history, a period of poly-drug use, a time in which people are hooked on the state of intoxication, on the feeling of being high. The poly-drug user craves drugs in general, any and every drug that will get him high. He may prefer a particular drug like alcohol or cocaine, even try to keep away from hard narcotics, but inside his own league he will take whatever he can get.

Poly-drug use started during the late sixties in the junior high schools. Kids curious about drugs took whatever was current and choice in the hallways. A suburban ninth-grader with a contact downtown would come to school one week with a thousand hits of speed, so the drug kids would be speeding for five days. Next week it might be blotter acid or marijuana, and if a week or two went by when nothing was available, the raids on father's bar or the medicine cabinet increased. This random use of drugs spread into every corner of the drug culture. The old street junkies in the ghetto complained that the young junkies had "no class," because when the heroin supply dried up the young guys would use anything.

What can you do about all this? You can begin by expecting one or more of your children to become *at least marginally involved with minor drugs no matter how good a parent you are.* I don't mean you should be breathing down the necks of each one of your children, watching for bloodshot eyes or slowed reflexes; quite the opposite. You may need to intervene some day, but to intervene effectively you will have to discipline yourself to step in, decisively, at the correct moment—not sooner, and not later. This means you will need to understand, even better than your teenager, the differences between the four levels of drug use. Understanding each one of these levels is more important than any other information you could possibly read about drugs. The first level is experimentation.

## EXPERIMENTATION

All young people are curious. High intelligence and curiosity are often blood brothers. The high school student who is entranced by the microcosm of life in a drop of lake water is also likely to be curious about the sensation different drugs will give him. To experiment means to try something out, to test it against what you have been told about it. The danger in experimenting with street drugs is that kids have no guarantee about the dosage or the purity of the drug. They can't even be certain that they have been sold the actual drug they wanted to buy.

LSD, which is used much less today than it was in the late sixties and early seventies, is still the most dangerous drug for an experimenting youth. Underground labs lace it with additives, some of which are poisons, thus making it physically dangerous. Psychologically it is unlike any other drug. It amounts to taking your mind into your own hands.

When John tried LSD at the age of sixteen, he didn't like it. He didn't have a bad trip—very few kids do—yet he didn't feel comfortable with it. "I just didn't like losing that much control." He never tried it again, and this is what is meant by experimentation. Kids who stay at the experimental level with a drug will try it once or twice and then drop it.

When Scott tried LSD at age fifteen, he loved it and felt none of the discomfort that John had experienced. "It was a marvelous drug. Instead of shutting down my brain, it left me perfectly unimpaired. I could see a new dimension, a new world that was always there and that I couldn't see before. It was inexplicably beautiful and amazing. For me, it was almost a religious experience."

Scott's experimentation led him into a prolonged LSD phase. He never had a bad trip, and two years later he stopped taking it because he felt he had learned all he could from it. "It's like Mescalito [the hallucinogenic power in LSD] is a strange guy," he explained. "You can use his power for only so long, and then he's shown you everything he can. That's when he decides you're abusing him—and then *he* abuses you."

Many young people never do more than experiment with a new drug, but if they move from that first or second try into a pattern of use, as Scott did with LSD, then they have stepped into the second level of involvement with drugs:

## CONTROLLED USE

Some people go straight from experimentation to abuse, but most, including young people, maintain control of their drug use. About ninety percent of all individuals, regardless of age, who drink alcohol or use other non-narcotic drugs are controlled users. If you have a cocktail or two before dinner every night, you are demonstrating controlled use. The weekend pot smoker is also a controlled user. When Scott decided he liked LSD, he became a controlled user: "I wouldn't drop unless the conditions were all right. I'd never do it indiscriminately."

In each case, the person takes a certain amount of his favorite drug—alcohol, marijuana, or LSD—and he often does so at the same time each day or each week. For the remainder of his waking hours he does his job, studies for classes, accomplishes life's goals. He does not allow the drug to control him. On the contrary, he controls the drug, he regulates the all-important trio of when, where and how much.

The controlled user always has a specific purpose for using the drug of his choice. He orders drinks before lunch in order to whet his appetite and enjoy an uninhibited conversation with a client or an old friend. He has a cocktail before dinner to relax with his spouse and forget the daily grind. He takes benzedrine so he can stay up all night and study for an exam or, if he is a truck driver, so he can stay alert on the road. He takes seconal to reduce the anxiety he has been feeling lately. He may smoke pot for the same reason, or simply to heighten his mood at a party. When LSD was most popular, many people took it in hopes of self-discovery. It was even used successfully in a few clinics to cure alcoholics.

Pleasure, relaxation, alertness, self-discovery, and the reduction of anxiety are all legitimate goals. It seems infinitely more desirable to me to pursue these goals without artificial help from chemicals.

But the observable fact is that a great many people in our society do use alcohol and other drugs, and that the majority of them can handle what they use without any problem. They are all "controlled users."

## ABUSE

How can you tell when a person has crossed the line between controlled use and abuse? Frequency is one major clue. And frequency is usually accompanied by the inappropriate use of a drug. The kid who smokes grass at a weekend party is a controlled user; the kid who gets stoned on his way to school is well into the abuse stage. So is the business executive who gets high and stays high from lunch right through the eleven o'clock news. Controlled use is appropriate use (except in the minds of teetotalers); it does not interfere with the work or personal relationships of the user. Repeated and excessive use of any drug quickly becomes visibly destructive to both the work and the relationships of the user.

You may be misled by a person who gets high in spurts. He is like a manic depressive. He will have several productive days, then lapse into a drug binge, then snap back and appear to be in control. He is playing a game with himself and with those who care about him, trying desperately to pretend that he doesn't really need to be high.

In fact, he doesn't need to be—not yet. He is abusing drugs. The motive may be a broken romance, a lost job, or a bad marriage. He may be having acceptance problems at a new school or feeling peer pressure to prove himself. He is teetering on the brink of dependence, but a good friend or a watchful parent can pull him back. He may not give up drugs entirely, but like the cigarette smoker who cuts down from two packs a day to one, he can and will do it if it is important enough to him. If he doesn't really care, or if someone doesn't give him a reason to care, he will go on to

## DEPENDENCE

Dependence is the opposite of controlled use. In the second level, the person controls the drug; in this fourth level, the drug controls the person. Ten percent of all the people who drink will eventually become dependent; five percent of all those who smoke marijuana will become psychologically dependent. The dependent person allows drugs to affect the quality of his work, the nature of relationships, future options, and the use of his free time. He will need professional help to stop, and even with that help he will have to regain enough self-respect to want the life that is possible to him.

## DRUG RISK

What kind of family is most likely to have children who will never touch drugs? Richard Blum and several co-workers at Stanford University have published a complex study of precisely this question.* They talk about "drug risk" rather than drug abuse. A "low risk" family is one in which none of the children uses any illegal drugs. A "high risk" family is one in which one or more of the children are compulsive drinkers or regular users of an illegal drug. In addition, if one of the children uses even small amounts of LSD, opiates, or cocaine, the family is considered high risk. Using these operating definitions, the following profiles emerge from Blum's research.

Low risk families are usually politically conservative and are traditional churchgoers. Father dominates the family, absolute obedience is emphasized, and the children have little freedom of choice. When asked to rank their values, low risk families put God and religion at the top of their list along with the earned respect of others. Freedom to go one's own way ranks last. Respect for the law is also emphasized in low risk families. Most such families believe all laws should be carefully obeyed, although some of them make exceptions if it is a law concerning traffic regulations, civil rights, or integration.

Mother is cooperative, encouraging, and humorous when she deals with her children; father is usually calm and didactic. Family life is active and full, and great value is placed on doing things together. The children usually have religious interests and demon-

* From the book *Horatio Alger's Children: The Role of the Family in the Origin and Prevention of Drug Risk,* by Richard H. Blum & Associates, © 1972 by Jossey-Bass, Inc.

strate self-discipline in their daily lives. They tend to follow their parents' directions without hassle, yet seem to feel that the choices they make are their own. Parents in low risk families believe they are rearing their children to be obedient, self-controlled, popular, and fulfilled people. If they fail to achieve this goal, the parents tend to blame external influences like bad friends and television.

High risk families are usually politically liberal and do not attend church. Their religion is science and reason. Neither parent dominates the family, and their stress is on tolerance, open-mindedness, and acceptance of change. When asked to rank their values, they rate personal happiness most highly along with self-understanding and the fullest possible use of one's potential.

Parents in high risk families are often ambivalent about authority. They tend to regard policemen as intellectually, personally, and morally inadequate, and see no reason to obey laws which they consider obsolete or laws which apply to drugs like marijuana. The parents dislike using power to discipline their children. They often try to run their families democratically, treating their children as equals. Family life is minimal, however, because parents and children alike go their own ways, involving themselves in community activities that capture their individual imaginations.

The children are often pleasure seeking, independent, and interested in left-wing politics. Parents in high risk families want their children to become loving people, and hope they will be flexible— prepared for life in a changing world. If they fail to achieve this goal, the parents tend to blame the child.

Mothers in low risk families are more likely to be job holders; mothers in high risk families are usually better educated. High risk mothers often feel a personal disappointment over the difference between what they are and what they hoped to be. They are also more likely to be dissatisfied with their children.

When a teenager in a low risk family is caught using drugs or when he gets into some other form of trouble, his parents sit down with him to talk over the situation and decide on a punishment. Their goal is to work out the problem without calling in someone from outside the family. If the trouble continues in spite of the punishments, the parents will blame neither the child nor themselves. They will be convinced that influences outside of the family are the causes of all the trouble.

Ironically, parents in high risk families are more likely to call the police if they find drugs in their teenager's room. They are deeply disappointed that their democratic child-rearing philosophy has failed to produce a responsible young adult. Tending to be uncertain of how to act authoritatively toward their teenager, when they feel he is out of their control they call in society's most obvious authority figures.

What do children from these two very different types of families turn out to be? Low risk families produce most of our solid, conservative citizens. High risk families produce most of our innovators, our skeptics, our liberals and radicals.

I feel ambivalent about this study because I feel a kinship with certain characteristics in both types of families. I don't want my children to depend on drugs, but I do want them to be free to go their own way and develop their own set of values. I like families who do things together, but I don't like parents who insist that all of their children join them on a vacation when one or more of the kids doesn't want to go. I believe that parents should provide their children with structure and guidance and that they should follow through with consequences when rules are broken; I don't believe that any family should be so bound by rules that an oppressive, inflexible atmosphere dominates everyone's life.

I don't know where you see yourself on the continuum between low risk characteristics and high risk characteristics, and in many ways it doesn't matter. To intervene effectively if one of your children becomes involved in drugs, you will probably need to adjust your values and train yourself to go against a few of your natural instincts.


## INTERVENTION

Most parents want to intervene either too early or too late in the drug process. Parents in high risk families may wait too long and allow their teenager to reach the dependency level before they act decisively. Low risk parents will want to step in dramatically at the first hint of drug use. Both actions can have unfortunate consequences.

When a teenager experiments with liquor or street drugs, he may feel some guilt because he knows his parents would disapprove, but he also knows that he is far from being an addict. He feels in control of his actions and does not consider himself to be "on drugs" when he has merely tried one of them out. And in all of these respects, he is absolutely right: he is not on drugs, he is not an addict, and he is in control.

That is why your intervention will often backfire at the experimental level of drug use, particularly if you respond with massive restrictions. For example, Sally smoked marijuana at a party with her boyfriend; it was her first experience, and looking back she thought it was "okay." She wondered why so many of her friends thought it was such a big deal. Her parents overheard a conversation in which she mentioned her experience, and because Sally's family is a typical low risk family, they sat her down for a long talk.

Compared to her brothers and sisters, Sally had always been a scamp. She had refused to let the family sand down her rough edges, had insisted on the right to choose her own friends, and gotten away with it because she is so energetic and artless that she won her father's heart. But the marijuana scared her parents. Considering what they had heard and read, they were understandably frightened and felt that Sally should be forced to see their side. They blamed her boyfriend for leading her to drugs and ordered her to stop associating with the kids who had been at the party, a group which included most of her closest friends. They reminded Sally that they had never approved of her most recent friends, and warned her that marijuana could easily be the beginning of a bad pattern; they wanted to nip that pattern in the bud.

Sally's personality changed overnight. She became sullen, moody, and irritable; she refused to eat and stopped taking care of her appearance. She told her parents they were "stupid" to make her stop seeing her friends. "I haven't done anything wrong! I didn't even like marijuana all that much!" But out of resentment, she started getting high with her friends at school. She knew she was doing it to spite her parents, but that seemed a good enough reason at the time. When she was finally caught, Sally's grades were well below her usual average and her relationship with her parents was a shambles. They blamed her friends for everything.

What should Sally's parents have done? Their natural instinct was to confront her, and it was not only proper but important for them to do so. They could have asked why she had wanted to try marijuana, they could have told her how strongly they disapproved of the use of any drug, and they could have asked her if she planned to smoke marijuana again. Sally was not the type to abuse drugs and she might even have promised to refrain completely in order to put her parents at ease. Instead, her parents' harsh demands provoked a major showdown. To Sally, they were asking her to give up her entire way of life: her friends, her boyfriend, her passion for independence.

Sally did not enjoy rebelling against her parents—she loved them too much for that. She knew she could never have the life she wanted without the support of her mother and father; even if she could have it, it wouldn't mean much to her unless they could appreciate and share in her accomplishments. The frustration and conflict she felt drove her to seek the limbo offered by the very drug to which she had been so indifferent. She is back to normal today, but her story helps show that when you overreact to drugs, you take the same chances that you do when you underreact.

Intervention can be helpful if a teenager reaches the controlled use level, but once again, it should be intervention with an open hand, not a closed fist. Dave's parents discovered that he was smoking marijuana regularly and using amphetamines occasionally during his senior year in high school. They insisted that he see a counselor, and I met with the family twice. Dave was an honor roll student, he worked part-time after school and had a regular girl friend whom his parents liked. He felt his parents were wrong to be so upset about his drug use.

"Why do you feel they shouldn't be worried?" I asked.

"I go to school, I make good grades, I get to work on time every day, and I don't smoke dope in school or on the job. I even do my chores around the house. . ."

His mother arched an eyebrow.

"Well, most of the time I do." He paused, anxious not to lose his point. "Some days I have to be reminded two or three times. But I do all these things *and* I smoke dope with my friends. I like it, and I don't see anything wrong with it."

"Would you give it up if your parents asked you to?"

"They already have—and I won't. I don't see any reason to because I think they're wrong."

"What about getting arrested?" put in his father. "Even if you can handle the drugs you're using, they're still against the law. You could wind up in trouble with people who won't listen as patiently as we do." Dave's father is a lawyer.

"I'll take my chances."

We did a lot of talking, but the session was a stalemate if our only goal was to get Dave to obey his parents' wishes. He was completely honest with them, and deep down they knew he was not the type to let drugs become a substitute for the goals he had set in his life. He *really could* handle it. And that's the way it was left.

If Dave's parents had tried to stop him from seeing his friends, he might have left home; as it was, the two sessions between Dave and his parents cleared the air and allowed for a full discussion of everyone's fears and opinions. The sessions also made Dave more aware of the anxiety his drug use caused his parents, and deliberately or otherwise he began cutting down on his pot smoking.

Forceful, direct intervention *is* essential if your teenager ever reaches the abuse level. Tom's parents knew he had crossed the line from controlled use to abuse because his behavior became so predictable. He left home every evening right after dinner to join a small group of friends. Together they smoked grass, drank Ripple wine, and joked the night away. Friends for years, they enjoyed each other, and most of their evenings were superficially pleasant. Still, Tom knew he was only doing it because neither he nor anyone else could think of anything better to do.

He leveled with his parents when they confronted him. Like Dave, he insisted that his marijuana marathons were not hurting him. But unlike Dave, Tom's drug use *was* hurting him—and his parents were prepared with specifics. "You once cared about studying medicine, but now you can't even get yourself to a simple job on time. You seem to have given up on college. You talk about putting in applications, but in another month it will be too late for the fall term. You don't seem to care about anything anymore except getting high with your friends." Tom thought they were being pushy and over-dramatic even though he knew it was all true.

The confrontation might have ended there, as such occasions

often do—a concession by Tom that his parents had a point, and a plea from them that he change his ways. If it had stopped there, Tom might have gone back to his nightly dates with euphoria; as it was, his parents literally forced him to come to my office. They didn't drag him in physically, but they did let him know they were prepared to do so if necessary. If you dislike the thought of using force, verbal or otherwise, you should understand that Tom would never have gone to a counselor unless his parents had brought him in.

I noticed Tom's sense of humor first. He has a true gift, a comic eye. He made fun of himself and of the world as he saw it, but always in a gentle, fundamentally compassionate way. Like many good humorists, he is an acute observer of human nature. I had no idea what his ambitions might be that first day we met, but I knew he would make a superb psychologist.

He was candid about his drug use. "I know I'm probably wasting my time gettin' off every night, but I like to do it and things are pretty dead around here anyway." He wasn't apologetic, but he was beginning to wonder what else life had to offer, and he showed a keen interest in joining a training group for people who wanted to learn group process. In the following weeks he became the most active member of that group, and his visits to the old gang dropped seventy-five percent. Within two weeks he had moved from the abuse level back to occasional controlled use, and he did it simply because he wanted to do it.

Abuse is not dependency. Lots of young people who reach the abuse level as Tom did are able to get off drugs because they get too busy to use them. Tom didn't give up marijuana entirely, but he stopped letting it interrupt his life. Outpatient counseling provided all the reinforcement he needed, and his parents were able to get him involved with me because they waited for the right moment. If they had badgered him day after day during the earlier stages of his marijuana use, he might have come to see them as his enemies. Every carping comment cements another brick into the growing wall between you and your teenager. You can discuss drugs with him if you think he is experimenting, and you should speak your mind—for your own sake as well as for his—but never let yourself become his enemy, because the day may come when you will have to be his only real friend.

Perhaps half the kids who reach the abuse level are very different from Tom. They will fight like tigers to keep from dealing with their problem. Verbal confrontation will fail. There is no way to resolve the situation without using physical force. And if that is what it comes down to, then when you are sure that your teenager is sabotaging his own life with drugs, it is time to *carry* him to a treatment center. A person who is forced into treatment has just as high a chance of getting well as a person who volunteers; in fact, sometimes the cure rate for involuntary patients is higher.

If you hesitate at the last paragraph, consider this case history described by Blum: "In one family, a young teenager was a problem, displaying extreme drug use, truancy, and an uncontrolled temper. The family called the older sister home from college—herself immature but marginally adjusted; she was to be the parents' consultant, and the younger child was placed in her hands. The sister unexpectedly advised that the thirteen-year-old should not be burdened with having to rule the whole family (the diagnosis she made) and suggested the parents do that job themselves. The parents then packed off the older sister and sent the problem child to a residential school instead—a school known for its permissiveness. This gesture failed too, and so the child was boarded with another family. That also failed. The next step was to give the child free rein; the parents paid for travel and expenses, while the teenager, by now fifteen years old, roamed the country on her own." *

It is easy to hesitate and to search around for soft alternatives; it's hard to face the truth and to compel your son or daughter to face it with you. Most young people who abuse drugs do not have to be dragged into treatment; many are quite willing to deal with their troubles and are only waiting for someone to show a sign of genuine caring. A minority will have to be given ultimatums like a choice between residential treatment and a juvenile detention center, and others—a very few—will have to be put into the family car and driven to an adolescent psych ward. Any of these solutions is better than becoming an addict.

---

* From *Horatio Alger's Children* by Richard H. Blum & Associates.

## RESIDENTIAL TREATMENT

Treatment in a mental health facility or a live-in center is necessary and good for a teenager who is drug dependent, but the same treatment can be downright harmful for a teenager who is a controlled user or even for a kid in the abuse stage. The harm or good depends on the philosophy of the treatment center. Some centers are controlled by counselors who were once chemically dependent themselves. They assume that everyone who touches a drug is just as weak as they were. They will interview a teenager who is a controlled user, a teenager who has all sorts of problems that have nothing to do with drugs—parent problems, school problems, peer problems, sex problems—but the counselors will ignore all of these other problems and focus all of their attention on the drug use. They will say, "Nothing can get better until you quit drugs." Hundreds of kids are turned off that way and never get any help for any of their problems as a result.

If you think that one of your teenagers is at the abuse level or even the dependency level of drug involvement, you can learn a great deal by visiting one or two of the drug treatment centers closest to you. If your son or daughter does go into treatment, make sure that the center's goals are clear. A counselor who believes that everybody is on the road to chemical dependency may be very good for a teenager who really is drug dependent, but he will assign everyone at his treatment center the same label: "dope fiend." Like the alcoholic who is told that he will always be an alcoholic even after he has been dry for years, the drug dependent teenager is told that he will always be a dope fiend even after he has been straight for years. I don't agree with that tactic, but it has been effective for Alcoholics Anonymous and it seems to be equally effective in centers working with drug dependent youth. At the same time, no young person who is not actually dependent should have to live for the rest of his life with a label like "dope fiend."

Three to six months is the average minimum stay in a residential treatment center. Many centers will return a teenager to you drug-free in that amount of time, and there are fringe benefits as well. Kids learn group process in the centers, and often become sensitive counselors for their own peers back in the high schools. But as a parent, you should insist on a time limit for any therapy: some kids get addicted to it.

## THE FUTURE

A person's time is his most valuable possession. People who are drawn to drugs are the very ones who should never touch them. But people of all ages are spending a lot more time high than they once did. It may be Ripple wine and a couple of joints, or it may be vodka martinis at the Ben Jonson Bar, it amounts to the same thing: more people than ever are getting higher than ever. This is a plain, observable fact.

Drugs and the conditions which inspire people to use drugs are not about to go away. As the hysteria that surrounded marijuana subsides, more people will try it and some will be converted. Most of them, along with most of the people who drink, will never have any drug problems.

The majority of this country's alcoholics are still men, but the most common drug abuser is now and will continue to be a white, middle-class housewife, age thirty-five or older. She uses too much of a non-controlled narcotic named Darvan. She is very quiet about it, but she is there—she will still be there twenty years from now. You can see her today, see her clearly, forecast in the words of this girl who today is only fifteen: "School is a drag, my boyfriend is mainly interested in my body, and my parents have got their own trip to do. I do dope because it's the one thing I can count on: it never lets me down."

# 9

## The Jesus Movement

Jill found only spiritual emptiness in her parents' church. She was seventeen, lonely, religious, and consumed by her need to belong somewhere, to be accepted. This made her a perfect candidate for the Jesus People, who met her one day in school and took her in.

Shortly after she "found the Lord," Jill bought a used car; it was her high school graduation present. She looked over the selections of several dealerships with her new friends, together they picked out a nice-looking compact, and Jill arrived home full of enthusiasm.

"We found a good car! The man says I can have it today, but you'll have to come down to sign the papers, Mom."

"Shouldn't we have a mechanic check it over first?"

"Oh, don't worry, the Lord will take care of that!"

Her mother took a deep breath and let it out without speaking. She knew it was useless to argue. Ever since Jill's conversion, the Lord seemed ready to take care of everything. So Jill picked up the car, drove it to a friend's house, and there several experienced Jesus People "prayed over every part" with her. Two days later the car broke down; repairs were over $350.

Before Bob, sixteen, joined the Jesus People he had three loves: a girl named Jeannie, a Gibson guitar he had saved for two years to buy, and springtime. He liked everyone he met and the feeling was always returned.

Today you can't get near him without hearing a sales pitch. He is selling Jesus, not vacuum cleaners, but it's hard to tell the difference. "No other model will do, and if you buy this one *now*, it will take care of all your problems for life!"

Bob has warned his parents that he fears for them because they are not born-again Christians. He is unimpressed with their thirty years of active participation at the local Congregational church. "Church people haven't given themselves one hundred percent for Jesus," he explains. "They're just religious hypocrites." Bob thinks his parents will go to hell unless they make the same kind of commitment that the Jesus People make.

He has left his guitar untouched since he found Jesus. His group approves of music, but Bob sees the guitar as a symbol of his former, worldly self. Drugs are another symbol of his former life; he had experimented with marijuana and LSD. Today he tells people on the streets that Jesus got him down off drugs. His old friends wonder how to get him down off Jesus. Even his parents, who are conservative Christians, liked him better the way he was before.

I approach this chapter with acute discomfort because I believe that one's faith is an intimate, personal thing. My faith includes Jesus, but equally important to me are acts of love between people or the union of spirit that I feel looking at a wild flower swaying in a high mountain breeze. In my bible, all of these things speak of the same God. Each person's faith has its own special chords and stanzas, and if yours include some notes similar to mine, it also includes many others which are uniquely your own.

But I hear the Jesus People say, "You are wrong and we are right. We have the One Way." My natural inclination is to feel sorry that they are missing so much, yet that is precisely the emotion they feel for me, and so we are strangers—even though numbered among them are people like Jill and Bob, who once were my friends.

Parents are sometimes frightened when their children join a branch of the Jesus Movement. Drugs scare parents because so little is known about them and because their power is real; the Jesus Movement scares many parents for exactly the same reason.

## WHO ARE THEY?

Southern California is the Galilee of the Jesus Movement and Hollywood is its secular capital city. The pioneers of the movement wanted to cast their seeds on fertile rather than fallow ground, so they converged like lemmings on the one part of America that offers the largest, densest collection of burnt-out freaks, drag queens, aging hippies, and miscellaneous crazies. That was in 1967.

The movement quickly became a scattered horde of competing groups ranging from moderate to radical. Four traits joined them in common purpose: their youth, their fundamentalistic belief in the literal truth of the Bible, their belief that total acceptance of Jesus as Lord is the One Way to salvation, and their universal conviction that the world is a sinking ship from which as many passengers as possible should be saved.

Jesus People really believe that they are the last generation that will live on earth. That is why the motto in some groups is "Forget education, forget parents, and forget work!" There is no time left for anything other than winning souls to the Lord. Many kids in the movement are scornful of the institutional church. To them, ministers have failed to see the imminence of the Last Days, and so they are like naive porters, rearranging deck chairs on the *Titanic*.

The fastest growing group of Jesus People is the Children of God. They live in colonies spread across the country in at least a dozen major cities. When parents complain that their children have been kidnapped and hypnotized by Jesus People, they are close to the truth; the Children of God, a more radical group, use high-pressure tactics to gain converts. They begin by insisting that new converts break all ties with their parents, husbands, wives, and other relatives or past friends. They base their insistence on Jesus' words in Luke 14:26: "If anyone comes to me and does not hate his own father and mother and wife and children and brothers and sisters, yes, and even his own life, he cannot be my disciple." (Jesus' meaning is clearer in Matthew 10:37, a synoptic parallel of Luke's hyperbole; Matthew records Jesus' words as "He who loves father or mother more than me is not worthy of me.")

A Children of God convert must donate all his possessions to his colony and the elders then sell what they get to support their work. All members believe they are the only true followers of God left on earth. They are openly hostile toward less radical Jesus People, who are described by one Child of God as "lukewarm pukes." If they have a frustrating day on the streets, Children of God occasionally "smite" an unbeliever with the Word of God, which means to hit him in the head with a King James Bible.

Despite their extreme tactics, the Children of God present

themselves publicly in joyous song fests and testimonials. They have won over some of the most intelligent and charismatic leaders from less radical groups in the movement. These leaders were turned off by the ego-tripping and the commercialism of the movement as a whole; they were also impressed by the staying power of the Children of God. One girl explained that although the Jesus People in her city won thousands of converts every year, they lost more than half of these newcomers within months. The Children of God lose less than fifteen percent.

What type of teenager is most susceptible to the conversion tactics of the Jesus People? Many actual converts are kids who hit the end of the rope, who tried all the new trips and found them wanting. Others are religious fundamentalists who feel guilty because they have failed to surrender their lives one hundred percent to Jesus. Many of them, like Jill, have a strong need for a sense of belonging, a need which is fulfilled by the colony and by the endless prayer meetings, study sessions, and witnessing sessions. Still other kids in the movement grew up in permissive homes and were left with a need for direction and discipline. The movement is good at providing both.

Several old organizations sit on the fringes of the movement, sharing its theology but lacking its spontaneity. They are groups like the Campus Crusade for Christ, Youth for Christ, and Young Life. They hire professional ministers and staff people, they sponsor rallies, and they are often recognizable by their slick ways and their preacher tone. But they do represent the establishment right wing of the movement just as the Children of God represent the radical left wing.

In between the extremes are hundreds of unpublicized splinter groups, and a few of them have produced the movement's real saints. They operate houses which serve as meeting places, provide crash pads for runaways and a free meal for those who need one. During a morning prayer meeting a young man is encouraged to overcome his past tendency to be violent and selfish; the leader tells him that "God can take what you were and turn it into an opportunity for good." While fundamentalistic theology is still predominant. the kids will admit that they are still looking for answers.

These kids begin to see that their relationships are not merely horizontal but vertical as well, that what they are is more than the sum total of their blood and bone and body chemistry. With this new dimension in their lives, they will either return to their families, join their comrades on the streets collaring converts, or they may be guilted into joining a more extreme group in the movement.

You may wonder, "Is this really a good thing for my child?" Some parents go to extraordinary lengths to rescue their teenagers from Jesus colonies; other parents are saddened by the loss of contact they have with their teenagers after conversion to the movement. But many parents do gratefully drive their children to group meetings of local Jesus People. For my part, I see both some good news and some bad news in the movement. First,

## THE GOOD NEWS

Kids can be brutally cruel to one another. The plain girl with thick glasses is taunted by slender girls with a grip on popularity. Boys with enviable physiques mock the ninety-eight-pound weaklings—as if every kid didn't have enough trouble hanging onto his shaky self-esteem what with pimples and braces, too much or too little flesh, and all the chronic insecurity of adolescence.

The Jesus People offer the scorned fatty and the vexed beanpole a world in which appearance no longer matters. They also reach out to football jocks and loquacious cheerleaders, inviting them to look further than the limited popularity they enjoy in their smug world. A group of Jesus People will typically include a combination of winners and losers from the life they have left behind, and everyone gains from the lesson that looks, popularity, and material success are not ultimately important. "Even if you win the rat race, you're still a rat."

The intense emotional pitch of the movement has succeeded in curing hundreds of drug users, including people who were using Class-A narcotics. Many colonies boast several members who were once hard-core street junkies. Their mere presence is eloquent testimony to the power of the movement, though this power is hardly unique: the Black Panthers are equally successful at getting people off drugs.

On a simpler level, the Jesus People offer good clean fun. Their Friday night worship services are highlighted by live music and uninhibited singing; a colony will sponsor a pot-luck supper with scores of young people attending. Music is ever-present, proving that rock-and-roll and the pentacostal approach to religion were never very far apart. Many an observer has come to scoff and stayed to clap and sing.

The Jesus Movement at its best does give young people a keen sense of direction in a world which tempts its youth with too many poor choices. The vigor of the Jesus People stands in sharp contrast to the dusty banalities droned from the pulpits of too many established churches. The movement takes young people, spins them around a few times, and then commissions them with a set of marching orders: the world is about to end, you are now among the saved, and your sole mission is to win as many others to Jesus as you can before The End.

## THE BAD NEWS

It is a personal matter, but I have lost a few good friends to the Jesus People. I am saddened that no open lines of friendship are possible between people in the movement and people like me, whom they consider unconverted. We are never able to sit down for a normal, friendly conversation. The hard fact is that once an old friend is solidly in the movement, he is interested in me not as a person but as a potential convert. Everything he says is directed toward the single purpose of persuading me that I am wrong and he is right. This zeal to convert among Jesus People is, in part, a direct result of their belief that the world is coming to an end, that there is no time left for socializing with unbelievers.

This End Game philosophy strikes me as the most dangerous aspect of the movement. The girl who was planning to work toward a career in law or urban designing suddenly gives up all her former aspirations because such work would make little difference with The End so near. Many Jesus People deliberately suffocate all of their best intellectual tendencies. To quote the words of a leader in the Children of God, "Education is all just shit." So if they go to college at all, it is usually to convert their fellow students, not to get an education. They could be right, of course—The End might be coming soon. But if they're wrong, we will soon have a large army of disillusioned, uneducated, and futureless adults.

The movement is also paranoid. Jesus People think that when The End comes, enraged unbelievers will persecute, beat, and kill them. Many kids in the movement believe they will die as Christian martyrs. When a Jesus Person is throttled by a gang of delinquents (usually because they got tired of listening to his spiel), the incident is recorded as further evidence that The End is near. Most colonies are extremely suspicious of visitors. If a stranger asks a few pointed questions or shows signs of training in theology, the newer converts are shooed out of the room like small children and the experienced elders spar with the stranger until he has had enough.

As time passes it tests the kids who left drugs behind when they found Jesus. Many of them go back to drugs. The movement tries to hold onto its drug converts by keeping them constantly high on Jesus. It is as if they have gone from one drug to another, and their faith is being sustained by daily shots of spiritual adrenalin. For most Jesus People, faith is a taut straight line from conversion to The End; any lapse is a cause for serious prayer, meditation, and communal support. In this way, everyone is kept as close as possible to a state of perpetual divine readiness.

But faith is not a straight line—it is more like climbing up a dragon's back. The greatest saints were men well acquainted with profound doubt, not only before they were converted but throughout their Christian lives as well. Jesus People get no training in the ups and downs of faith; instead they are taught that faith is a hundred-yard dash. But when that pace is sustained and drawn out day after day, many kids wind up just as burnt out on Jesus as they once were burnt out on drugs.

Theologically, there are big differences between the Jesus of history and the movement which has taken his name. Many Jesus People, though certainly not all, behave like the biblical Pharisees. The Pharisees were outraged when Jesus casually ignored several old religious laws; he had collected grain and healed a man on the Sabbath—acts strictly forbidden by law. When the Pharisees challenged Jesus and asked him for an explanation, he answered, "The Sabbath was made for man, not man for the Sabbath."

Like the Pharisees, many Jesus People are legalistic, elitist, and full of public piety. These are attitudes which Jesus himself fought against. They are also the attitudes which eventually nailed him to a cross.

Finally, Jesus People believe that the world is divided between the Forces of Light and the Forces of Darkness. This belief, known historically as the Manichean heresy, originated in Persia during the third century. It is a combination of pagan and religious elements from that era. Like the Jesus People, the Manicheans felt it was their mission to wander the earth bringing people the Truth. Their thoughts were governed entirely by one book, the writings of their prophet, Manes. They believed that they, as vessels of the Truth, were the only particles of Light in a world overwhelmed by Darkness. They told everyone they met that they had the One Way, and they died out more than five hundred years ago.

These are times when you need a sense of humor just to make it sanely through the day. In the spring of 1974, streaking was the new campus fad, and the police looked the other way because they understood, perhaps better than any of us, how desperately we all needed a good laugh.

That is an insight not often shared by the Jesus People. Their humorlessness is just as fundamental as their theology, despite the façade of happy singing and beaming smiles. Their vision of The End, of the final separation of the sheep from the goats, is as cold and fatal as the gaze of a Nazi at a death camp: unbelievers won't be herded into ovens—they will burn in hell.

I wish the movement had a few gifted self-critics, a few leaders willing to go beyond the emotional, charismatic spontaneity that started it off. Maybe this is impossible; a dash of reason might destroy the movement. But as it stands, the Jesus People are riding a steam engine with limitless fuel and no brakes, heading down the tracks toward a Second Coming which may not oblige the time schedule they have so confidently imagined.

No one in the movement is willing to train its members in a more open, less static faith, to look at the dragon's back and say,"That is where we must go." The leaders refuse to take into account the lessons of history and biology, partly because the liberal churches have already tried that route. Besides, there is no time: we are already in the Last Days. If some kid is a dope junkie one day and a Jesus junkie the next, praise the Lord! Who cares that his mind is still the mind of an addict? He will experience divine rapture soon enough, and until then his brothers and sisters can give him his daily Jesus fix.

Parents who are upset by the movement must understand that, with rare exceptions, they are not dealing with a rational force. A certified Jesus Person is impossible to outmaneuver on his own turf, and he will refuse to play on yours. He is playing by different rules than the rest of the world and is certain that his rules are His rules.

The New Testament disciples thought The End would come in their own lifetimes. Jesus himself had said so, or at least the disciples thought he had (Mark 9:1). As they got older and a few of the early followers died, people adjusted their expectations and prepared for a longer wait. Out of this waiting came the church.

Unless they are right about The End, today's Jesus People will get gray from waiting and witnessing, and they too will adjust their expectations. Their message may mellow a bit, and organized groups like the Children of God may become new denominations with full bureaucratic regalia.

The sad losers will be those kids for whom the movement is a last hope. Like people in the old west, they listen to the medicine man and buy his snake oil. The label says: "Forget education, forget parents, and forget work." They get high on Jesus and win souls to the Lord and soon they will get old. They may never discover that their last hope was a false hope; that they were conned out of the best years of their lives by people who misused the power of the Name they spoke so glibly; that we have all lost something because of what they were never able to give to life; and that they are left with a little-e end, victims of a spiritual swindle.

# 10

## Staying Together for the Kids

"In a way, I'm glad they separated, because when they were together they were hell to live with." Those words belong to a sixteen-year-old girl who knows what it's like to spend years—impressionable, growing years—living with parents who do not love each other.

Most people assume that divorce is bad for children, that unless two parents are clawing at each other's throats, they should hide their unhappiness and stay together for the kids. It is a common assumption, and no one knows for certain how many parents follow it, parents who might go their separate ways if no children were involved. But we do know that staying together just for the kids can be a dangerous mistake. An honest divorce is better for children than a dishonest marriage. Of course, even an honest divorce is extremely painful for parents and children alike. No matter how considerate or creative two separating parents try to be, divorce is always hell.

But there can be a worse hell. It is the emptiness and the indifference, the strain and the sadness that fill the air in a home where father and mother no longer share the affection which originally brought them together. It can be a worse hell than divorce itself because in too many families, the sadness goes unattended and seems to have no end. Young children usually know—and teenagers *always* know—when a marriage begins to go bad. Nonetheless, many parents try to hide or deny or ignore the truth; as a result, uncertainty begins and grows and finds no resolution. The kids wait for a sign of hope or a final denouement, and it is this waiting and the insecurity which goes with it that does them the most harm. After years of emotional divorce, a legal divorce is often a relief for everyone.

None of this is easy for me to say because all of it affects me personally. I am a father, and I have been through a divorce. I know that as I write, I may select and present only those facts which justify my own past actions. On the other hand, I may be so wary of reaching a self-serving conclusion that I tiptoe around the evidence and say nothing at all. I feel content to go ahead with what I have observed and let you be the judge.

Parents in Minneapolis often asked me if I could see any pattern in the home lives of teenagers who came to me for counseling. Were most of them from permissive homes? strict homes? broken homes? That question started my staff and me on a careful check of back records and current clients.

We felt immediate frustration. What, after all *is* a permissive home or a strict home? Everyone has his own definition. We did find one unique pattern which startled us: most of the teenagers we had counseled were convinced that their parents were unhappy together. Their perceptions were sometimes right and sometimes wrong; the important point is that they acted on what they *believed* to be true, and their actions had usually gotten them into trouble. In many cases, the problems which these teenagers had in their own lives could be traced back to the insecurity and the tension caused either by their parents' unhappy marriage, or by the young person's belief that his parents were unhappy.

Teenagers are natural romantics. They fall in and out of love, they are full of passion and compassion, and they are true believers in the power of romantic love. When they sense that this kind of love is missing between their parents, it worries them because no teenager wants to see his parents break up. If he thinks they are drifting apart, and if a sorcerer could grant him a single wish, he would use it to wish that his parents might be happy together. But in the absence of magic, many young people go into the marriage-saving business.

## JOHN: DIVERSION

Most kids are sincerely afraid of a frank face-to-face talk in which the subject is their parents' marriage and the two other participants are their own mother and father. Because of this fear, some teenagers use a classic military strategy: they create a diversion. Set off a few explosions on the left flank to draw "the enemy" away from the main battleground.

For John, the enemy was not his parents themselves but the bickering that dominated their relationship and the affair he knew his mother was having. His purpose was to get them talking about something different, to force them to concentrate on his troubles rather than their own troubles.

As an inexperienced troublemaker, John began his diversion strategy when he was fifteen by throwing a rock at a passing squad car. The rock hit, but the officers merely ignored it. Frustrated, John waited a week, got loudly and illegally drunk, and threw several large rocks at a parked squad car on which two policemen were leaning at the time. That got him the results he wanted: he was taken down to the station where his parents were duly notified, a warning was issued, and the case was dropped.

John was persistent. Over the next three years he was caught shoplifting, drinking, or skipping school on dozens of occasions. He often timed his misdemeanors in order to be sure he would be caught; once he lit a marijuana cigarette in the men's room at school because he knew a teacher was on his way in to check the place for smoking. It was all a conscious, deliberate strategy, and it failed. John's parents had so little left between them that they were unable to act in concert to help their son.

The police never took John into juvenile court because they knew why he was causing trouble and tried to make friends with him. One of them begged him to stop playing games.

"You've got to start thinking of yourself for a change. Your folks will either make it or they won't make it, but the way you're going you'll go down the tubes whether they do or not."

The policeman suggested to John that he level with his parents, confront them with his feelings and ask them to get help, but John refused. "I'm not too good with words. Besides, if I bring all this up they might just fight worse than ever."

John paid a high price for his efforts. Most of the parents in his neighborhood refused to let their sons and daughters associate with him and it was a lonely three years. The fact that he kept trying for so long testifies to the importance young people attach to their parents' happiness.

John might easily have destroyed himself in an attempt to save them. Instead, he changed dramatically during his senior year in high school; he took the cop's advice and decided to think about himself. He worked to pull his grades back up, stayed away from home as much as he could, and found a girlfriend—the first romance he had ever allowed himself. Today he is in college working on a psychology major.

It would be nice to end the story right there. But John still feels the pain generated by his parents' unhappy and as yet unresolved marriage. "I hate to go home because when they're both in the same room, everyone gets tensed up. And my sister Carey, she's starting to pull all the same crap I did. She's only fourteen and I've tried to warn her it's no use, but she just acts like she doesn't know what I'm talking about. She's already worse than I ever was."

It is common in homes like John's for the younger children to pick up the "responsibilities" dropped by the older children, including the job of being a diversion for mother and father. Unless the source of family tension is dealt with, there will always be at least one child in trouble, trying to be a lightning rod for the family's pain.

## HOLLY: CONFRONTATION

Holly set off louder explosions than John did and was much less aware of why she was doing it. Her mid-teen years show how the tensions of a bad marriage can drive an adolescent in half a dozen different directions, all dangerous.

She ran away from home twice before she was sixteen, was arrested once for possession of LSD and hashish, used those and other drugs heavily, and went through an unwanted pregnancy and an abortion just before her seventeenth birthday. The only part of her life that went well was school; she graduated fifth in a class of five hundred.

Her parents had given up on each other when Holly was ten, and they had adopted a "you go your way and I'll go mine" attitude, living separate lives under the same roof. It was all very civilized. The bitter in-fighting which provoked John to take action was not part of family life at Holly's house. Her parents were also both staunch Methodists, and having an affair was not their style.

"Sometimes I wish one of them would have an affair," Holly once told me. "Maybe that would force them to make a decision." For her, the hardest thing to take was the artificial mood she felt whenever her parents were together. "I love them, but they're so phony, always putting on an act for other people and for us kids, trying to pretend that everything is fine. All of us know it's bullshit."

"All of us" included Holly's older brother and two younger sisters. When Holly's own troubles leveled off during her senior year, she was nominated to take a message to mom and dad. If it's true that you aren't happy, the message said, please get someone to help you decide what to do—and don't worry so much about us.

When Holly asked for a conference, her parents assumed she must be in some new kind of trouble. She remembers feeling more nervous than ever before in her life and it took her a long time to get to the point. But as her parents slowly understood that she was talking about *them*, about the effect of their relationship on her and the other children, they tightened up and her father cut in.

"This is none of your affair, Holly. What's between your mother and me is for us to work out, not you. If you want to talk about your rules or other matters that affect you personally, we'll be glad to listen, but we won't have any more of this other."

Nothing more was said on the subject for over a year. Then one afternoon, alone with her mother on a shopping trip, she got this glimpse into why her parents had stayed together:

"I know you think your father and I should separate, and I think I understand why you feel that way; I was a girl once myself. But we have spent a lot of years together, and these last few years we've tried to settle for what is possible. It may not look so great to you, but maybe we aren't as unhappy as you think."

Later that day Holly resolved to reach for much more in her own life than what is merely possible. She had come close to understanding the reality of her mother's words, yet the insight left her with an empty feeling, and with a melancholy determination to do better.


## LAURIE: RETREAT


While John tried to divert his parents from their marital troubles and Holly tried to talk to hers, Laurie called a retreat. She identified closely with her father, loved him deeply, and didn't understand what had made him such a terribly unhappy man. All she knew was that her parents acted as if they were cool and distant relatives, rarely talking much between themselves. She had once asked her father what was wrong, but he laughed off her questions and told her not to worry.

In fact, during her high school years, Laurie's father was an unadmitted alcoholic. He ate breakfast in silence, shielded from the rest of the family by the morning paper; he went to work, a job to which he gave both wisdom and skill; and he came home at night to stare for hours into the color television and drink himself to sleep.

I know this is depressing to read because it is depressing to write, but living through it is spiritual suicide. To protect herself, Laurie borrowed from her father's script and built a wall of her own. She used drugs and indifference for bricks, and silence for mortar; she quit high school in the middle of her junior year and once tried to kill herself. In the end her parents got a divorce, but by then Laurie had built so many defenses around herself that no one could reach her, at least not for very long.

Laurie, Holly, and John are not the exceptions in homes with unhappy parents, they are the rule. Several studies using careful scientific designs have confirmed the danger of staying together for the kids once a marriage is spiritually over. One study compared "unhappy, unbroken homes" with single-parent homes and normal two-parent homes. Children from the unhappy, unbroken homes showed a higher rate of delinquency, they had more problems with adjustment and personality development, and they had more psychosomatic illnesses than any of the other children.

By contrast, children living with a divorced parent were similar in every respect to children from healthy two-parent homes. In fact, many children living with divorced  mothers tend to participate more actively in family problem-solving and learn the value of a dollar more quickly than their friends from normal two-parent homes.*

I certainly don't want this chapter to sound like an advertisement for divorce, but I do want to counteract the notion that divorce is always a terrible disaster for children. The evidence is that both young children and teenagers can absorb the shock of a divorce and adjust well to a new and different life. If the love between mother and father has dried up, family life is like crossing an endless Sahara without water, and in the end everyone loses.

## MAKING IT WORK

Every story has another side. The other side of this one is that some parents are good at living with a bad marriage. They work hard to present a calm exterior; they learn to be content with the challenges of their work and with the pleasures of watching their children grow up in an intact home. Their children may sense a vague distance between mother and father, but they find the distance hard to define. Even when they know their parents have lost any romantic feeling for each other, the kids may appreciate the hidden decisions which keep the family in one piece.

Jan, seventeen, and Jason, fifteen, are part of a family which lived that way for years. Then suddenly—or so it seemed to the kids—their mother asked their father to move out for good. There was talk of divorce, and both Jan and Jason were determined to prevent it if possible. You'll be happy to know that this time, everybody won.

Both teenagers became angry with their mother when she refused to explain why she had finally called a halt to her marriage. She was determined to keep her children out of the issues which had

* From "Characteristics of Adolescents from Unbroken, Broken, and Reconstituted Families," by Lee G. Burchinal, *Journal of Marriage and the Family*, February, 1964.

led her to seek a divorce, issues which went back more than ten years. As she told a friend, "I won't defend myself and I won't criticize their father."

You can probably imagine yourself reacting the same way. Few parents want to share with others the more intimate feelings they have had as husband and wife, especially not with their own children. But Jan and Jason were determined to be included, to be told why the break was necessary. "This is our family too, and if you and dad get a divorce it affects us—we're involved already!" Their insistence got only superficial reasons from their mother, reasons which heightened their frustration. As Jason said, "She hasn't told us anything yet that I feel is a good reason for throwing Dad out." Jan agreed.

Jason visited his father in the furnished apartment he had rented, and Jan got her mother aside to beg her to be more open, to help them understand. Then the kids switched parents, Jason talking with their mother and Jan with their father. With each parent they shared news of the moods and feelings of the other, and gradually both parents opened up—against their own better judgment—allowing the teenagers to serve as conduits of information and feeling. The kids left no doubt that what they wanted most was a reconciliation, but they resisted the temptation to push for that goal; a divorce would be fine too if it was the only solution. Both parents were deeply affected by the actions of their children, and definite talks of a divorce stopped. They began to think about staying together and called on a marriage counselor to help them sort through the issues.

The teenagers welcomed their father home two months later. Many of the old habits were buried, and their parents' relationship had moved ahead to a new phase which included a renewed affection. The family had won, and it was a good place to make a new beginning.

Every marriage sooner or later gets stuck between a rock and a hard place. Getting unstuck often requires a little blasting powder, and teenagers may notice the explosion but miss the purpose behind it.

We saw a lot of teenagers at my agency who *thought* their parents were unhappy together, but not all of them were right. The sad part is that unless their parents were willing to set them straight, those kids often followed patterns similar to the ones taken by John, Holly, and Laurie.

I have a good friend who, at twenty-nine, has made his way through several short-lived love affairs. When one of his romances gets down to the hard work which is the basis of any enduring relationship, he always backs away. As his last amour was foundering on stormy seas, he grinned and told me, "I think I like the infatuation stage of a relationship best of all."

Any marriage which has lasted long enough to produce teenage children has long since passed from the infatuation stage to the work stage. I don't mean that to sound dreary. A couple's commitment may be deeper, the sex may be better, the enjoyment of a spring evening richer than ever; but if all those things are true, we can be sure it took some hard work.

Young people are well acquainted with the infatuation stage and are relatively unschooled in the work stage. They watch you, they notice the quality of your interaction, and they sometimes mistake the work of keeping a marriage together for a lack of spontaneity and romance. If you think I'm suggesting more open communication between you and your teenagers on the subject of how mom and dad feel about each other, you're right. If that kind of talking happened more often, this chapter could become irrelevant.

The best way to have healthy children is to have a happy marriage. The other side of that coin is also true: the best way to have disturbed children is to have an unhappy marriage, and to let it go on and on and on.

# 11

## Living Together

A giant insurance company based in Chicago told its salespeople that in 1975 as many as half of their best potential customers would be young men and women who were unmarried and living together. The rapid increase in the number of couples who defer marriage for a while in favor of living together is a fact no one disputes, but the morality of what those couples are doing is a matter of considerable dispute. It is a subject, like politics and spinach, on which people of good will are unlikely to ever agree. According to a recent survey, about one-quarter of the American population think cohabitation is just plain living in sin; another quarter think it's a good idea; and fully half of all Americans feel that if a couple wants to live together, it's nobody's business but their own.

Last year, during a climb up Long's Peak in Colorado, I met a young man and two young women who all argued that marriage was on its way out, that it's a useless old custom no one should take seriously any more, and although it may have served a valid purpose at some point in history, that purpose was no longer in evidence. Their feelings are echoed by many of the high school students I have met in recent years, most of whom say they intend to live with a lover before considering marriage. The most insistent young people are those who feel that their own parents have had an unhappy marriage and those whose parents have been divorced, but the idea of living together is a strong one in teenagers from all kinds of homes.

Despite the obvious trend, very few parents approve of an opposite-sex living arrangement that involves one of their own children. They usually find it a difficult subject to discuss because it's such a total contradiction of every moral law they have ever believed. If that reflects your own view as a parent, this chapter is written partly with you in mind. It is not intended to argue one side or the other, but to look hard at love and marriage, at the reasons why some young couples think that, like oil and water, love and marriage don't mix.

## WHAT'S WRONG WITH MARRIAGE?

In my role as a minister, I have presided at scores of weddings, each one of them unique. I always ask the couple to write their own vows and, if they wish, to select the readings for other parts of the ceremony. I want them to think about why they love each other, why they are making this commitment, and what they hope to do with it. I want to be sure that their wedding is a pure reflection of what and who they are and of where they want to go. The mother of the bride always thinks that this process is too loose, that the service will be too unorthodox, that the words should come straight from *The Book of Common Prayer*. But once the ceremony is over, she is always the one who thinks it was "just perfect" because it was "so much like them."

Many of the couples I have married recently are couples who lived together first. It may be only coincidence, but invariably they are the couples who write the most profoundly moving vows. They seem to bring an awareness and maturity to the altar, a clear-eyed understanding of the strengths and the weaknesses they will take with them into their future life. I asked each of them why they had waited to marry, why they had wanted to live together first, and I got some very interesting answers.

First, almost every couple admitted that they were scared stiff of marriage in the early days of their courtship. Like most of us, they knew someone who had been through a divorce—a friend, a relative, sometimes a parent. They knew that the chance of a successful marriage is getting more risky every year, that the failure rate for marriages between people under the age of twenty-five is three times higher than the overall rate, that teenage marriages are almost always disasters.

A Washington psychologist estimates that for every marriage that ends in divorce, there is another marriage that stays together unhappily. If he's right, then less than half of the marriages in America today are happy ones, and the state of California is in real trouble—the divorce rate there is fifty-fifty. Whatever the truth may be, many young people have already seen more than enough to make them afraid of marriage.

The brides gave me a second clue to the reasoning behind living together before marriage: they had often suggested the arrangement in the first place. They wanted more from life than the role of housewife and mother and felt that marriage often reduces the woman to a subtle but real second-class status. They were frightened by the image of the jobless wife in her late forties, her children grown and flown, who looks into the mirror and asks, "Is this all?" The unanimous answer of the young brides with whom I talked was "Not for me!" Although many older mothers will say that these young women have a distorted picture of the life of a wife and mother, it is that picture—distorted or not—that makes many women today think twice, and twice again, before putting on a wedding ring.

A third reason for hesitation about marriage is time. As medicine combats disease with increasing success, "till death do us part" gets to be an awfully long time. The couples I married felt it was reasonable to take some of that time, a year or two at the beginning, to learn whether a lifetime commitment made any sense.

Not surprisingly, the parents of these same couples were unimpressed by the all-too-reasonable approach to marriage taken by their sons and daughters. They wonder what is wrong with the Old Way—dating, courtship, separate quarters, engagement, and marriage. If time is needed for sorting through the pro's and con's, why not settle for a long engagement?

"So you get engaged," countered one couple. "That usually means you're spending all your spare time together, you're going to bed with each other, but you're sleeping for a few hours each night in separate places to keep up appearances. What's the difference between that and living together, except that living together is more honest? And it's a better test of your relationship."

Most parents do assume that sex is a major factor behind any couple's decision to live together. In fact, when a couple is ready to talk about sharing living space, their sex life is usually as active as it will ever get; what they want to find out is how they will get along in other ways.

Many couples move in together simply because they get bored by the carefree, swinging life that Old Marrieds remember as so glamorous. If you've ever been to a college mixer or to a singles' bar, you know they don't wear well as the months slosh by. Free sex and free love are actually quite different, and too much of the former can get self-hatingly bleak, particularly for people who dislike superficial relationships. Many living-together arrangements grow out of a wariness of marriage combined with a longing for something which has, if not permanence, at least a measure of truth.

## THE SHOTGUN WEDDING

A few of the couples who lived together and then came to me wanting to get married should have stayed the way they were. Steve and Linda are one such couple. They are both twenty-six, they lived together for two years prior to their marriage, and they were under constant pressure from their parents during every month of those two years. Their parents refused to come visit them because to do so would seem to sanction the relationship. Both mothers often asked, "Have you two thought any more about getting married?"

But Steve and Linda were happy as they were. They felt a strong commitment to each other, were almost sure they would stay together for life, but they were suspicious of marriage. Steve spoke for both of them when he said, "We don't need a piece of paper to give meaning to our love. I think what we're doing really means more this way, because no law is telling us we have to stay together. We're together because we want to be."

When, several months later, Steve asked me to marry them, I asked why the change of minds? "Because it would please our parents," he said. "So we feel, why not? It won't make much difference to us one way or the other, but it will make a big difference to them."

I should have said, "That's not a good enough reason to get married." Instead, I encouraged them to write their vows and think about the kind of service they wanted. It was a nice wedding—everyone said so—but it seemed just a few degrees off to me, the kind of service in which most of what is said and done is for the benefit of everyone present except the bride and groom. It was a sophisticated version of a shotgun wedding.

The consequences were quick in coming. Steve and Linda were in trouble within a year of the ceremony. Steve had noticed a new insecurity in Linda. "She's more possessive now, always wanting to know where I am. She hates to see me go out for a beer with a friend. All I know is, she never used to be like this."

Linda's side of the story was a familiar one. "We seem to fight most of the time these days. Steve spends more time with his friends than he does with me. When we were living together, *I* was one of his friends, but it isn't that way anymore."

That problem is hardly unique. Many couples have to face it and work out a solution to it, and a healthy couple usually can. But Steve and Linda blamed the change in their relationship on marriage itself; it was *marriage* that was bringing them down and pulling them apart. They had not willingly chosen to marry, they had not taken the added risk of marriage out of the well of their own common hopes; instead, they had married to quiet their parents and to end their own sense of guilt, a guilt fed and stoked almost daily by parental intervention. Steve and Linda are now divorced.

"Shotgun" weddings can be caused by extremely subtle pressures, not all of which come from parents, but young men and women with a high respect for their parents are very sensitive to parental reaction. They want neither to hurt nor to be hurt. If they begin living with someone, they will want an honest reaction from you, a complete reaction if possible, and they hope it will not be one of total disapproval. You should beware of inadvertently guilting your children into a marriage that might be ill-timed or ill-conceived or both. I have several hat-in-hand recommendations aimed at preventing such inadvertences.

## A STRATEGY FOR PARENTS

1. If your son or daughter announces an intention to live with a prospective mate, take time and give your own reaction without holding anything back. If you disapprove mightily, say so. When you try to swallow your disapproval, it tends to come back up, get stuck in the throat, and color your words with condescension. Most young people prefer outright disapproval to condescension. If you have a negative reaction to the idea of cohabitation, talk over your reservations with your son or daughter. It will help to clear the air and both of you will know where you stand. You may discover that you approve of living together if and when it touches your family personally, and if approval is your reaction, be sure to share it.

2. Keep out the welcome mat no matter what your feelings are along a scale of disapproval to approval. Send a dinner invitation, or if they live some distance away encourage them to come for a brief visit. If they do show up for a live-in visit, use your own rules under your own roof. If your values say separate bedrooms for unmarried people, make sure the message is clear. One mother, whose son had lived with his girlfriend for two years, assigned them to adjoining rooms when they came for a Christmas visit. "I'm giving you two rooms," she announced upon their arrival, "and what you do with them is your business."

3. If you think your son or daughter has bad taste in romantic partners, keep quiet about it. Some day you may be asked for your candid opinion; if so, give it—simply and spitelessly—and explain your reasons why.

4. Give them all the space they need to make up their own minds. When two people are trying to decide a question as life-involving as marriage, they don't need outside agitators, especially when the agitators are their own parents.

The death of God was a big deal in the late sixties, and the death of marriage is a big deal in the middle seventies. Some people think that by 1980, the only people left who will still want to get married will be Catholic priests.

However, marriage seems to be holding its own with young couples. One of the couples I married told me a year later that since the ceremony they had gotten to know each other far better than they ever did when they were living together. I was pleased, and I asked why. "I think we feel more vulnerable now," the woman said. "The stakes are higher, the risk we have taken is more real, but we aren't afraid of it. Now we take chances with each other we never would have taken before—and with each chance, we grow."

The poet Theodore Roethke once said, "Those who are willing to be vulnerable move among mysteries." Mountain climbing, deep-sea diving, and racing fast cars are all one kind of vulnerability. They each bring a person face to face with the possibility of his own death, and in so doing they can give life a richness and a texture it could not otherwise have. Marriage is another kind of vulnerability, one in which we take the risk of closeness and commitment. That, too, is a risk which can add a unique richness and texture to life.

We can each afford only a limited number of serious investments in hope during one lifetime. Young people are looking hard these days for something to believe in. Many of them are finding out that the best possibility is also the oldest one, the coming together of two people who risk believing in each other, and in so doing learn what it means to move among mysteries.

# 12

## Twenty Tips to Parents from Parents

In this chapter parents speak for themselves. I asked ten parents from different families—six mothers and four fathers—to share what they had learned during the years their children were teenagers. Two of the women are now grandmothers and two others reared their children alone; some of the parents still have children in junior high school.

Between them, these ten parents have brought up thirty-eight children. Without exception their sons and daughters have distinguished themselves in high school or in college, or both. But before this time of achievement, the parents and one or more of their teenagers endured a time of trial: a son arrested for drug use, a daughter who ran away, a serious argument over appearance or priorities.

Although the parents I surveyed have never met each other, many of their ideas and suggestions were unanimous. I have left their words unchanged, and many of the paragraphs that follow contain sentences and phrases contributed by six or seven different people. In what they say, these parents and their children bring an old dignity and a new style to the words "mother," "father," and "youth."

### 1. Set as few rules as possible. Then, stick to them!

Make sure your rules aren't just arbitrary, and try not to get into battles over trivial issues. Arguments over jeans really aren't worth the grief. Save your anger and ammunition for an *important* issue! Every fight, every nagging word makes the next one less meaningful; eventually you're tuned out completely with the main event not even on yet. Say "yes" to your kids as often as you can because there are "no's" too. Your "no's" will mean more if you have mostly a "yes" point of view. Try to avoid ultimatums, even though it's not easy to do. If your ultimatum was unrealistic to start with, it is hard to enforce and harder to take back without looking silly.

### 2. Expect your rules to be tested.

If your family standards are based on deep convictions rather than day-to-day caprice, your kids will be more likely to respect them. But growing children *must* test the boundaries of behavior around them. If the family provides no boundaries, they will test the boundaries of society wherever they can find them, because test they must. How much better to test the boundaries established by those who care for them! Try to keep in mind one thought: this testing is a plus, even though it may cause you some discomfort and concern when it happens.

### 3. Listen!

Try not to fall asleep when they're talking! It really hurts a child's feelings if you are too busy to listen—like having a long, long phone conversation or sitting in your favorite chair reading the paper when they come home with something to say. So when they do talk, listen and try hard not to interrupt.

### 4. Respect their privacy.

Nothing is more upsetting to teenagers than to have their privacy invaded by parental prying—listening in on phone conversations, reading mail, inspecting desks and drawers. Let your kids know that their privacy is as important to you as it is to them. You may have some anxious moments sticking to this rule if you have reason to be suspicious about something, but resist the urge to snoop. If you resist that temptation your efforts will pay royal dividends later in life—in the respect your children will have for you, knowing that you always respected their dignity.

### 5. Maintain the generation gap.

Don't try to be part of their world: it's theirs, not yours. Teenagers resent parents who try to be part of their world almost as much as they dislike adults who entirely reject their world. You can avoid this resentment by defending your own ideas and values in discussions with your teenagers, even when they collide with the values held by your sons and daughters. Just remember that standing up for your own views does not mean forcing them on your kids.

### 6. Don't moralize!

Teenagers often have a different standard for what is or is not moral. Nothing turns them off faster than hearing you preach to them after they've made a sincere effort to share an opinion of their own, particularly when you repeat the same message again and again. You'll get further with them when you find a way to say what you mean minus the "preacher tone."

### 7. Let them work out their own life styles.

Try for healthy compromises. For example, you might insist on cleanliness but not on short hair for your boys; if it's clean and out of their eyes, count your blessings. Don't hold up someone else's son or daughter as your idea of a "good kid." And if you have a teenager who shows an early desire to go his own way, try to keep long-range goals in mind. An early exhibition of independence can be irritating, but if you can see independence as the goal you want in the long run, the incident becomes a positive part of growth.

### 8. Try not to make promises that you can't keep.

This is a hard rule, but if you do have to break a promise, try to have an excuse that is valid in your teenager's eyes. If you can't convince yourself you have a good reason for saying "no" to a former promise, you'll never convince your kids. If you do have a good reason for changing plans, it will be tough on the kids—but maybe before too long you can find a way to make it up to them.

### 9. Don't try so hard to communicate.

If you're trying that hard you're probably failing anyway. The kids will only look at your efforts as nagging, prying, criticizing, and worrying pointlessly. What you *do* will communicate itself far better than your attempts to use Dreikurs, Ginott, Harris, or whomever you've read lately.

### 10. Expect good, and you may get it.

Enough said.

### 11. Don't worry when they don't talk.

If they tell you practically nothing about what they're doing, so what? If he tells his secrets to his friends, he's normal. If he tells them all to you, it's time to worry about him because that's not normal! All it takes is a little recollection of your own younger years and you'll soon stop expecting to be "told all," or even much of anything.

### 12. Enlist the help of your older children in understanding the needs of your younger ones.

When you're troubled by the growing pains of a fourteen- or fifteen-year-old, ask your older children for advice and counsel from time to time. It's a marvelous way to bring them into your thoughts, to gain an understanding of your younger child, and to give some solace during the rough periods.

### 13. Admit you're human and make mistakes.

Your children might as well hear it from your lips. Surprise them by apologizing if you've been wrong about something you said or did. When you can show a teenager that you are not inflexible or dictatorial, you may find him relying on you more, not less.

### 14. Be available when they need you.

So what if you miss that special television show or are late to a party or have to drive twenty miles to take your kids to a meeting, picking up four of their friends along the way. They will be so grateful, and you won't be troubled by guilt pangs when you go off and do something for yourself, leaving them behind.

### 15. Don't get caught in the middle.

Don't be the one your teenagers come to with a secret they don't want your spouse to know. You must weigh your communications with each member of the family, and a conspiracy of silence against either father or mother is difficult to live with.

### 16. Let your children be children.

How many times have you heard a parent say, while talking about his three-year-old son, "Now that Johnny knows so many words, we're working on correcting his grammar and pronunciation." Parents who say this don't really like children. To please them, Johnny should have born at the age of thirty!

### 17. Be patient.

Let your children make their own mistakes, within reason, and accept their failures as not only forgivable but as a necessary learning process. It may be hard to see your kids fail because it's easy to think of their failures as your failures. They'll learn what you want them to if you give them the space to win and lose on their own.

### 18. Try not to condemn.

A particularly independent teenager may press you to your limit, but if you can keep extending offers of help and at the same time refuse to condemn the decisions he makes—even when you disapprove strongly—he will come back to talk with you more readily in later years. Whatever else you do, don't despair during the noncommunicative years.

### 19. Let your children know that they mean everything in the world to you.

When you feel proud of them, give them the praise they deserve; support them and let them know how pleased you are. They need and want to be loved and respected—by you—whether they realize it or not. They need to hear, "I love you, no matter what."

**20. *Just keep telling yourself: "Soon, it will be all over!"***

Have faith, because it's true!

It was impossible to compress all the humor and the richness shared by these ten parents into twenty short "rules." Being a parent of teenagers is, in many ways, the hardest part of parenthood. One of the fathers who contributed to a great deal of this collection, whose own children are now all over twenty, summed up the final reward: "Today our kids, secure in their own responsibilities, independence, and significance, are returning home as though it were a mecca. This returning is the complete fulfillment of parenthood."

# 13

---

# Finding Help When You Need It

One study of people who seek professional help for personal problems shows that half of them get over their problems while they are still on a waiting list to see a therapist. In other words, therapists would have a fifty percent cure rate if they would just leave their potential clients alone. We could call it waiting-list therapy.

People often do get better after they have taken the risk of asking for help with a problem. Just *asking* means that you have taken two of the most important steps toward a solution: you have recognized the existence of a problem and you have decided to do something about it. The third step is more difficult, but if you will take it you have a good chance of solving all of your family problems without outside help.

This third step is the recognition that if any member of your family is in trouble, then the whole family is in trouble. When a parent has problems, the family has problems too. When a teenager is in trouble, his entire family is in trouble. The best help for any problem involving a family member always comes from within the family. But it is often hard to get everyone together at the same time and even harder to get everyone to agree that if Johnny is having problems, they aren't just *his* problems but something for the entire family to work on.

We are all tempted to make the family troublemaker into a special case, a bad seed, a child lured into mischief by irresponsible friends or by some flaw in his own personality. We are, quite naturally, never anxious to acknowledge the possibility that something we have said or done has contributed to, or even created the behavior we deplore.

In the Brown family, for example, fourteen-year-old Bob is the only one of four children who has ever gotten into any serious trouble. He runs with a pack of other junior high boys who are believed to be the cause of dozens of vandalous acts in the neighborhood. Bob himself has been picked up by the police three times; once for theft, once for drinking, and once for public obscenity. When any adult tries to talk with Bob, he either keeps a stony silence or starts making caustic remarks.

Bob has an older sister, Pam, a senior in high school. She is known as a leader and her numerous awards and achievements are a source of pride for her parents. But Bob feels that Pam is too stuck up and bossy, at least in the way she relates to him.

Then there are Jim and Susan, ages twelve and ten respectively. They have plenty of friends and rarely argue with their parents. Jim is his father's pride and joy, a raw-boned natural athlete, rangy and powerful for his age, the kind who could grow up to be a professional tight end. Now that he has reached junior high school, his father expects him to letter in three sports.

By contrast, Bob is slender, intellectually gifted but physically uncoordinated, a disaster on the ball field and a rather transparent disappointment to his father. And Bob knew it, too, at a very early age.

Little Susan understands the unspoken competition between Bob and Jim, but mostly she knows that Bob makes their mother sad and their father angry by getting into trouble so much. Susan loves her parents and hates her brother Bob for upsetting them.

So Bob is obviously the family problem, and if help can be found for Bob, you might ask why the rest of the family needs to be involved. After all, the other kids each have a life of their own and none of them is causing any trouble. But if you look more closely at the Brown family, you will see how everyone in it is helping, in some way, to keep Bob just what he is—a troublemaker.

Pam agrees with many of her father's feelings about Bob—that he is lazy, irresponsible, remote, and impudent. She is also privately glad that Bob is so unproductive because as such he presents no challenge to her role as the family's most conspicuous success.

Jim has mixed feelings about the praise he gets from his father; he likes the attention but wishes he didn't have to shoulder so many high expectations. He would like to spend more time on activities other than sports, but knows how much any sign of a lessening interest in sports would disappoint his father. Because of this, he has begun to envy Bob for his maverick role in the family and encourages him in subtle, non-verbal ways to keep it up. He knows that Bob may be breaking ground that he will want to travel himself in a couple of years.

Susan understands what is going on in the family but she feels there is nothing she can do about it. She and Bob were very close when they were both younger, and she has cried a few times over the loss of his affection. Bob is sure that Susan couldn't care less about him because she always sides with their parents, but he, too, is hurt by the loss of affection between Susan and himself. To hide his feelings, he pretends that he has no interest in what she thinks or does.

Mr. Brown pays attention to Bob only when he gets into trouble. Mrs. Brown, caught in the middle as so many mothers are, sees how the family has locked Bob into his rebellious position. At the same time, she wants to keep everyone as calm as possible so she hesitates to be the only one to defend him. Bob is highly sensitive to his mother's feelings, understands her predicament, but responds by behaving so hatefully around the house that he gives her nothing to defend. In this way, Bob adds himself to the list of family members who help to keep him the way he is.

The Browns are a *typical* family, not a special case. These same dynamics operate in every family, shaping personalities and leading in predictable directions. You can explore these interrelationships on your own, and once you have begun you have also begun a form of do-it-yourself family therapy. You may not ever need to ask a professional therapist to help you if you begin by asking each member of the family to help. At the same time, you should keep yourself open to the possibility that a counselor may be both needed and valuable.

## ASKING FOR HELP

Americans aren't very good at asking for help. Our tradition is one of self-sufficiency, of settling our family quarrels privately. This feeling is especially strong among men but it affects women too. The result is that we all feel vaguely ashamed and inadequate when we go to anyone else, a professional or just a good friend, to ask for help. We are also likely to let a problem reach the desperate stage before we begin looking for the help we need. We all accept the idea that preventive maintenance will help keep our cars from breaking down, but we won't accept the same idea for families, even though a family is much more sensitive and complex than a car.

Many parents feel that a call to a family counselor is an admission of personal failure. It is actually an attempt to confront family pain. The best counselors are often people who have had problems of their own, who have asked other people for help, and who have worked their problems through to a solution. They will never make you feel small when you ask them for help because even though they have a great many skills, they know it often takes more courage to ask for help than skill to give it.

Once you have decided to ask for outside help, you still face the question of who: whom shall you invite into your life and the life of your family? And an even more important question may be: whom can we afford?

If you are church members you might begin by asking your minister for a referral. He may have counseling skills himself, but unless everyone in the family likes him it is best to go to someone else. If your troubles are not extreme, it may be wise to delay any impulse to go immediately to a psychologist; there are several intermediate steps which could save you some money. Every large urban area has at least one community information and referral service. It is a central resource file, often funded by the United Way, which can tell you what agencies are closest to you, whether or not they are free, and something about how they operate.

The late sixties and early seventies spawned a large number of paraprofessional youth workers. "Para" is a Greek prefix which means "alongside of." Paraprofessionals often work alongside the psychologists and social workers in a city; they run drop-in centers and youth crisis lines, drug treatment programs and teen clinics. They tend to have a lot of street savvy, so they can be more effective with adolescents than an office-bound psychologist because they are able to establish trust so quickly. You may have people like this working right in your community, and they could be your most valuable contacts. Even if it does turn out that your family needs a fully-trained family therapist, the paraprofessional worker can be a helpful bridge between you, your teenager, and the professional therapist. He will know if the problems in your family are complex enough to merit more expert help than he can give, but in many cases he will be able to give you enough insight to settle your problems without looking further.

Although federal funds have been cut back, some communities still have local mental health centers staffed by psychologists and psychiatric social workers. These centers were created to make professional counseling available to people with low and middle incomes, so clients are charged according to a sliding scale based on income; help is ready and waiting for as little as one dollar an hour and, in some cases, no fee is charged.

In some cities the best source for immediate help is the youth "hotline." Staff quality varies widely, but most phone services have energetic, qualified people who are interested in crisis intervention and in supplying you with the names and numbers of individuals and agencies that could be most helpful to you. Because these phone services are youth-oriented, they know which counselors and which agencies have the best record for working with teenagers.

Your local Youth Service Bureau is another good source of information about different kinds of help available nearby. You are likely to be astounded by the number and variety of services for parents and children, services you never knew about until you felt a personal need. Most communities have at least one good alternative school for kids who are doing poorly in regular school programs. Call the central administrative office to inquire. If you are a single parent and you work during the day, you may worry about what your kids are doing from 2:30 to 5:30 every afternoon. If so, the Manpower program in your area may be able to offer your teenager eight hours of work each week; the going rate as I write is $2.10 an hour with the chance of more than eight hours a week for kids who show a strong interest and the ability to learn. Many drop-in centers for youth also have good tutoring programs during the after-school hours. Make a few initial calls and you are sure to find the right agency and the right person to help you—believe me, it's true!

## HOW DO I GET HIM TO COME?

If the problem is one which requires counseling, you may be ready and willing to talk with a counselor but what if your son or daughter isn't buying the idea? Parents often call me, describe Johnny's problem in grim detail, express a willingness to come in themselves, and then add, "But how do I get Johnny to come?"

I used to tell parents that the old folk saying is true—you can lead a horse to water but you can't make him drink. I believed that you could ask your teenager to come with you to see a therapist but that you couldn't force him to come, and that even if you got him to come you couldn't force him to talk once he was there. I would tell parents that "a person must want help in order to be helped."

In a misleading kind of way, all of that is true. If a person has made up his mind not to talk with you, you can't make him talk unless you torture him, and if a person is willing to talk with you but unwilling to do anything to help his situation, he won't improve. But on another level, a person can be forced into therapy and make rapid strides. A person who is dragged through the doors of a counseling center can be helped just as much by a good counselor as the person who walks in willingly; in fact, the reluctant holdout may deal with his problems more quickly and more honestly than the eager volunteer. In short, the line I used to give parents may sound good, but it's just not true.

On one occasion a mother called to set up an appointment for her son, leading me to believe that he wanted to come in for a talk. On the day of the appointment she arrived outside my office with a struggling thirteen-year-old boy whose face was a portrait of anger. "This is *stupid!*" he was shouting. "I want to go home. I don't want to be here! *I'm-not-talking-to-anybody!*" His mother was thrusting him toward me and he was pulling back like a spooked colt. Before I could say a word, she shoved him through the door, yelled "Pick you up in two hours," over her shoulder, and disappeared.

I wish I could remember what I said in the minutes that followed, but it wasn't the kind of situation in which you switch on a cassette and say, "Why don't you tell me about it?" I do remember that I felt at least as uncomfortable as he seemed to be, and perhaps that common bond gave us a starting point. At any rate, he was talking so fast ten minutes later that I had to slow him down, and two hours later I had made a new friend. More important, my initially reluctant new friend was ready and anxious to try several ideas I had offered, including some sessions with his entire family.

I don't recommend that you drag your hesitant teenager to a therapist and shove him through the door, but I do believe there is no harm done when you compel a teenager to come, at least for the first appointment. Most young people, like most adults, picture shrinks as Hollywood caricatures with high foreheads and receding hairlines who sit back and say, "Um hmm. . . .yes. . . .uh huh," while you talk. It usually takes only one visit to dispel that picture and create an atmosphere of hope and trust.

## THERAPY JUNKIES

Too much counseling can be worse than none at all. Insecure, dependent young people can easily become therapy junkies, addicts who are unable to do a thing without talking first with their therapist. They will call him every hour they feel anxious, angry, sad, happy, confused, guilty, or just plain lonely. Some kids are seeing two or three people in the counseling professions simultaneously, and if one of their counselors refuses to support this dependent pattern they will dial the next person on their list. Extreme dependence is often natural in the early weeks of therapy, but in some teenagers the pattern goes on for years.

Youth hotlines always have dozens of dependent callers, lonely kids who sit in their rooms six or seven nights a week talking to the volunteers who man the lines. Some teenagers invent heavy problems in order to have a good excuse to talk with the better listeners.

They are not playing games with the crisis lines; their loneliness is real, but they know that we have not yet found a way to cope with simple and profound loneliness in our society. Since many urban areas have from five to fifteen phone services, these kids can spend all their spare time dialing one service after another—and a tragic number of young people do just that.

Groups are another form of therapy to which some people get addicted. I believe in groups. I think they are tremendously helpful to most of the people who join them; they can provide you with honest feedback about yourself, they can help you become more aware of your feelings, and they can energize your self-reflective powers. A group is an extremely powerful force, and it is this very power that leads some people to make groups an entire way of life. The problem with this, as one educator put it, is that although "the groupers are really honest and open, most of them have a lot of trouble dealing with ordinary people—policemen and longshore-men and average, everyday redneck, brownneck, blackneck Americans."

Many groups are well worth joining, but to keep from becoming a group junkie you have got to keep constantly in mind the fact that it is *only a group*—it is not the real world, and the way people behave in groups is not necessarily the way that people behave out on the streets. A group is a good place to experiment with new forms of behavior, with expressing anger or joy, sadness or love; but a group is something that you go to once a week, it is not a slice of real life. In a group you can say to yourself, "I really don't like that lady sitting over there," and you may be encouraged to express your feelings to her, but if you were out on the street you wouldn't walk up and tell her that you don't like her. If you did, people might say that you are honest and open, but they would also say that you are weird!

The best way to avoid becoming a therapy junkie is to make an initial contract and stick to it. You take your family into counseling for, let us say, eight weeks, and at the end of eight weeks you look at what has happened. You go in with a specific problem and at the end you take stock of your progress on *that specific problem*. You might want to make a new contract to work on a different problem, or you might want to renew the first contract for an additional number of weeks, but you never proceed on an indiscriminate basis.

The same rule holds true for groups. A good group has a time limit, and the best groups rarely run longer than ten or twelve weeks. It is good to learn how to end a group, and it is wise to limit your own participation in groups, as well as your teenager's participation, to well-spaced intervals. Going from group to group is quite the same thing as sitting in your room alone calling one phone service after another.

## UNCOMMON SENSE

I think that this book is mostly a book of common sense, but one thing I've noticed about common sense is that it's pretty uncommon in a crisis. The common sense solution is always the one we think of later, looking back on what we actually did.

One of my favorite heroines is a mother I have never met. Her teenage daughter came home late one night still a bit dazed by some barbiturates she had taken earlier in the evening. It wasn't an overdose at all, she could talk, walk, and make sense, but for some reason she didn't want to come in the house right away and go up to her room.

"I'll be all right," she told her mother. "Just let me sit on the porch by myself for a while."

And her mother said, "Okay." There was a lot of trust in that one word, "Okay." Maybe her mother sensed that the four walls of a bedroom would be too constricting just then or that somehow, going upstairs and getting into bed was a frightening idea for her daughter.

It seems such a simple act on mother's part, but think of what she could have done instead. She could have started a violent argument about drugs—as many parents have in similar situations; she could have insisted that her daughter go straight upstairs—as many parents have; she could have sat her down in the living room and given her a lecture—as many parents have. Instead she conferred trust at a time when trust was hard to give. Tomorrow would be time enough to talk over the why's and the wherefore's.

The fresh night air, the freedom to sit quietly, the time to let the numbness fade, all worked on the girl and did their job. Later she came in from the porch and went quickly to bed.

Now that was an uncommon, common sense solution. It sounds deceptively simple, but it required presence of mind, patience, trust, and love. Not one or two of those qualities, but all four of them at once. Together they made it possible for mother to say, "Okay."

## ONLY A MOTION AWAY

The solutions to so many, many family problems are only a motion away. An apology. An embrace. A handshake. A grin rather than a grimace. A heart-to-heart talk. And, if necessary, the dialing of a phone to ask an outsider for help.

If you have read this far, then I have been your guest for several hours off and on. I wish I could meet you as you have met me, because then we could share and sharpen ideas and, in so doing, make this a richer book. The world is small enough so that we might have that chance, but if not let me close with the hope that your love for those close to you and theirs for you will, time and again, reach the level of each day's most quiet need.